The craft of
NATURAL DYEING

To my father,
who taught me respect and wonder
for the natural world,
and my husband, Roger,
for his unfailing love
and support.

The craft of
NATURAL DYEING

Jenny Dean

SEARCH PRESS

First Published in Great Britain in 1994

Search Press Ltd
Wellwood, North Farm Road,
Tunbridge Wells, Kent TN2 3DR

Reprinted 1998, 2001, 2005, 2007

The Publishers would like to thank the World Conservation
Monitoring Centre, Cambridge, for their advice on
endangered trees and plants worldwide.

The author wishes to point out that some of the well-known,
old-established dyestuffs have been omitted from this book
because of concern about the conservation aspects of their use.
Similarly, some of the chemicals occasionally used in natural
dyeing have not been included because of the environmental
and safety factors involved in their use.

Every effort has been made to ensure the accuracy of the
information in this book and safety precautions have been
given where appropriate. Neither the author nor the
Publishers can accept responsibility for any injury, loss or other
damage resulting from the use of this book.

If you have difficulty in obtaining any of the materials
or equipment mentioned in this book, please visit www.
searchpress.com, or write for further information to the
Publishers.

Search Press Limited, Wellwood, North Farm Road,
Tunbridge Wells, Kent TN2 3DR, England.

ISBN 10: 0 85532 744 8
ISBN 13: 978 0 85532 744 6

Printed in Malaysia by Times Offset (M) Sdn Bhd

Contents

Introduction

The ancient craft of dyeing was practised by most early civilisations. Long before the advent of chemical dyes, peoples all over the world relied solely on nature to provide them with sources of colour.

Natural dyeing is gradually becoming rarer in many of the countries where it once flourished, so craft dyers in the western world have an important part to play in ensuring that the skills are kept alive.

Not every plant which produces a colour in the dyebath or on material will necessarily turn out to be a reliable or fast dyestuff, but most of the natural dyes covered in this book have stood the test of time. Once you have understood the basic principles and mastered the techniques, you will find that natural dyeing is not only quite simple but also extremely rewarding.

Nowadays, when concern for the environment has become important, there are several things which users of natural dyes should bear in mind, so remember to follow all the instructions in this book and take heed of the safety and environmental notes.

The joy of natural dyeing is that it is never boring, for you are always discovering new sources of colour. The excitement of finding, using and perhaps even growing your own dyestuffs never fades, nor the fun of creating endless variations of natural colour.

Materials

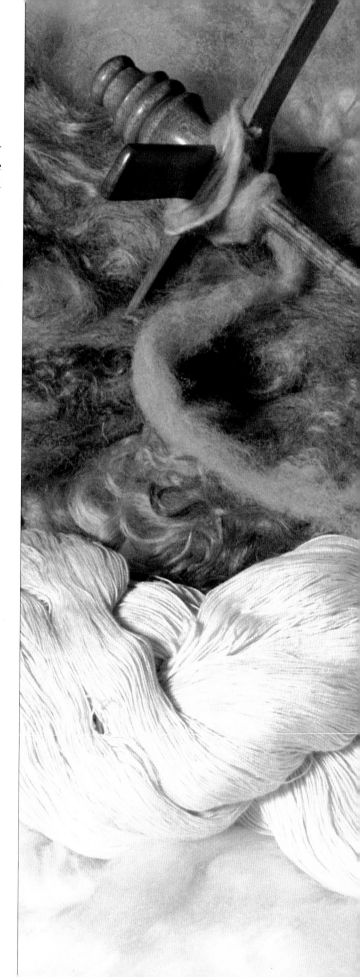

You will need some sort of fibre to dye (normally wool, silk or cotton); the *dyestuff*, which is the source of colour; the *mordant* – or fixative – (and assistant) to fix the colour; and water.

Fibres

Although some natural dyes will work successfully on synthetic fibres, in this book I shall be dealing with natural fibres. These can be divided into two distinct categories.

Fibres of animal origin

These include wool, silk, mohair, alpaca and several other less common fibres. All these fibres are based on proteins. Natural dyes are most successful when used on wool, silk and mohair, so most natural dyers choose these.

Fibres of vegetable origin

These include cotton, flax (linen), ramie, jute, hemp and many other less common fibres. All these fibres are based on cellulose. Some natural dyes tend to be less successful on cellulose fibres than on protein fibres. While the methods of dyeing both animal and vegetable fibres are essentially the same, the mordanting methods for the two categories are different.

In this book I refer mainly to wool or cotton, but in general you should treat other animal fibres as wool and other vegetable fibres as cotton.

Blends of fibres (wool and cotton types) can present problems. You may need to decide which of the fibres in your blend you wish to be dominant as far as colour is concerned and then mordant as for the fibre of your choice.

Some yarns may contain rayon or viscose (a type of rayon). Rayon is a so-called regenerated cellulose fibre and is made from wood pulp or chips. It may also be made from cotton waste. Rayon should be treated as for vegetable fibres.

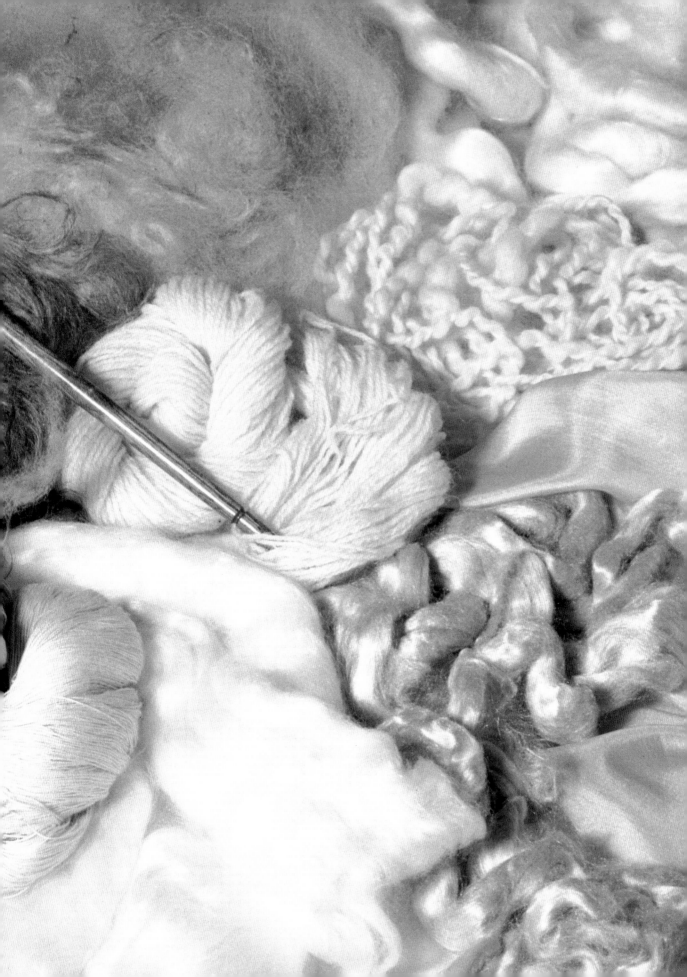

Dyestuffs

Many plants have a natural dye potential in their leaves, stems, flowerheads, berries, etc., and in the chapter on 'Dyestuffs' I have given details of the different categories and how they can be used.

However, your choice of dyestuff will depend primarily on the colour you wish to produce, and for each desired colour there are usually several possible dyestuffs available. In the chapter 'A world of natural colour' I have listed the recipes of dyestuffs and mordants that can be used to create particular colour ranges. It is often difficult to know which to choose, so consider reliability, availability, cost, and light- and wash-fastness.

The most environmentally friendly way to obtain dyestuffs is, of course, to grow your own, and I give some suggestions for this in the chapter entitled 'The dyer's favourites – some plants to grow'.

Some dyers prefer to use only dyestuffs which they can gather from their gardens or from the wild. Some stick to the ancient dyes, while others choose only those dyes which give fast, reliable colour (and not all do!). Most dyers probably choose a selection of dyestuffs from all these categories, depending on the results they are aiming for. If you do have to buy your dyestuffs, try to make sure that they originate from managed sources and have not been gathered from the wild. Most suppliers of natural dyes are responsible people and purchase stocks from renewable sources.

Mordants

The word 'mordant' comes from the Latin *mordere* meaning 'to bite' as in 'to fasten on to'. 'Assistants' are substances used with the mordants to help them do their job properly.

Mordanting is the process of pre-treatment of fibres which allows the applied dye colour to be permanently fixed. I describe this process in the chapter 'Dyeing a skein of yarn'.

It is just as important as the dyeing process itself, since careless mordanting will produce poor or patchy dyeing.

Various substances are used as mordants: some are perfectly safe, while others need more careful handling. In the chapter on mordants I give a number of different 'recipes'; I also show how the more harmful mordants can be used without presenting a threat to the environment.

Which mordant and dyestuff you use will be determined by the colours and shades you would like to produce and the material you are dyeing. You will find that a variety of shades and colours can be obtained from one dyestuff by mordanting the material with different substances. I also discuss this in the chapter on mordanting.

Water

Ordinary tap water will normally be suitable, although you will have to use rainwater when a recipe calls for 'soft water'.

There are no hard-and-fast rules for the quantities of water you will need. In general, you need enough to cover the materials being mordanted or dyed, and to enable them to move freely in the water. Remember to top up the water if it boils down. Too little water will result in patchy dyeing.

Different types of water

Some dyestuffs work better with a certain degree of alkalinity or acidity in the water, and it is useful to have a book of pH indicator papers available so you can test your water. Neutral will show a reading of seven; acidic waters will give a reading below seven; while an alkaline water source will be indicated by a reading above seven.

If your water is too acid, add a few grains of washing soda and retest, using a new pH paper each time. If it is too alkaline, add a few drops of white vinegar (or acetic acid) and retest. However, a specific pH reading is usually only necessary if you want to produce a particular shade or colour; unless the recipe states otherwise, use neutral water.

The effects of acidity or alkalinity

You should know how to adjust the pH of your tap water in case you need to: for example, if you fail to get a good result with a particular dyestuff.

In some cases, increasing the alkalinity of the water will bring out pink tones from dyestuffs that usually produce coral to purple colours, while increasing the acidity will enhance their orange tones. You could try experimenting with the addition of washing soda or white vinegar to the dyebath, but it is best to do this only on sample batches.

You should bear in mind, however, that washing soda, if used too freely, tends to make wool slimy. It can even rot, or almost dissolve, the wool, so be careful.

It is also interesting to note that, very occasionally, simple washing may cause dyed yarns or fabrics to change colour. This is probably due to excess alkalinity during the washing process, in either the water, the washing powder or the fabric softener.

It is often simpler, especially at the experimental stage, to use your tap water as it comes, as long as you are satisfied with the results.

Equipment

The equipment required for successful natural dyeing should be readily available in your kitchen; if not, you can get it cheaply and easily. To start, you will need the basic equipment below.

Heat source

A kitchen cooker will do, but as it is better not to use possibly harmful materials in the kitchen I do most of my dyeing in an outhouse, where I have a two-ring electric hotplate. You could also use a camping gas stove, or even an open fire.

Mordanting and dyeing pans

In general, you should use only stainless-steel or enamel pans. Enamel pans are less expensive, but make sure the enamel is not chipped, especially if they are second-hand. White enamel is useful as residues of dyes can be seen easily and cleaned after you have finished dyeing. Pans made from copper, aluminium or iron can affect the dyebath and produce a different colour from the one you were aiming for.

Look out for a second-hand stainless-steel or enamel boiler, as these make excellent mordanting and dyeing vessels, and have their own built-in heat source too.

Stirring rods

Glass or stainless-steel rods or spoons are best, as they do not absorb the dye. Stout wooden ones (simple wood or bamboo sticks) are quite adequate but you must use a different rod for each dyestuff or dyebath.

Thermometers

For some dyes the temperature of the liquid is crucial, so you will need a thermometer which has a range of 0 to 100°C (32 to 210°F). A long one is particularly useful, as the temperature at the bottom of the liquid, when this is on the heat source, is often hotter than at the top.

Jugs and jars

Some recipes call for rather precise quantities of liquid. Glass measuring jugs are best, but plastic ones will do, provided that they are resistant to high temperatures and can be cleaned out properly.

Storage containers

Dyestuffs and mordants need to be stored in a dry place and silica-gel sachets are useful for keeping mordants dry. Some mordants and dyes are light-sensitive, so dark glass jars or containers with a lid are useful. Alternatively, you can use plain glass jars and put them in large, thick brown-paper bags with a rubber band round the top.

Large glass and plastic jars are ideal for storing the remains of a dyebath which you want to use again for a lighter shade, but do let the dyebath cool down before transferring it. Some dyebaths may keep for several weeks, and if mould appears on the top, just remove it before reusing the dyebath. Some dyestuffs need to be soaked before use, and jars with a lid come in handy for this too.

Plastic bowls and buckets

You will need a collection of these to use for wetting the yarn or fabric before mordanting it, and for rinsing afterwards. Washing-up bowls are ideal. Keep a separate plastic bucket solely for indigo dyeing, as the blue stain can be difficult to remove from plastic.

Strainers

Once you have released the colour from the dyestuff, you will need to strain the dye solution to remove any solid material left in the dyebath. If the dyestuff pieces are large, a plastic colander is ideal; otherwise use a large plastic-mesh strainer.

Very occasionally a recipe will require you to leave the dyestuff in the dyebath, as the colour is released gradually during the process. To prevent the dyestuff from getting tangled up in the yarn (and causing patchy dyeing) you may prefer to place it in a muslin bag or a pair of old tights – but make sure these are dye-fast or you may have some surprising or undesirable results! The muslin will absorb some of the dye, so be sure to add its weight to that of the yarn or fabric before working out dyestuff quantities. Alternatively, you could put the dyestuff in a fine-mesh plastic net.

Scales

Throughout this book, where precise quantities are required, I have used the metric system of measurement for both liquid and dry substances. It will make things much easier for you if you can get a pair of special scales (from laboratory or scientific supply companies) for measuring small quantities, and these will inevitably be metric. If you do find it impossible to get metric scales you can use the guidance on approximate conversion from metric to imperial measurements given below. If you cannot get special scales, make up a mordant solution – it is probably the best method.

Imperial measurements

Dyestuff quantities

For 4oz of material to be dyed:

100 per cent dyestuff	= 4oz
50 per cent dyestuff	= 2oz
25 per cent dyestuff	= 1oz

(30 per cent would be around 1¼oz.)

You would have to use a bit of guesswork for other quantities!

Mordants and assistants

The quantities given are per 4oz dry weight of material to be dyed.

METHOD: make a mordant solution by dissolving 1oz of the appropriate mordant in 40 fluid ounces of very hot water. Cool and store in a dark bottle. (See page 28.)

Quantities of mordant solution

For 4oz of material to be dyed:

Alum	14fl oz	*for wool*
Cream of tartar	12fl oz	*and silk*
Alum	40fl oz	*for cotton*
Washing soda	10fl oz	
Tannic acid	10fl oz	*for cotton*
Copper	4fl oz	*for all fibres*
Iron	4fl oz	
5 per cent dilute acetic acid (or white vinegar)	2fl oz	
Also:		
Oak galls	2½oz	
Sumach leaves	2oz fresh	*for cotton*
	1oz dried	

PROTECTIVE EQUIPMENT

You should get *all* the following items before you start, *and remember to use them* throughout the dyeing process.

Pan-holders

Insulated pan-holders or a pair of oven gloves will be useful when you are handling hot mordant pans and dyebaths.

Apron

Always wear an apron to protect your clothing, preferably a plasticised one.

Rubber gloves

Some mordants and assistants are irritants, while some are even toxic, so always wear rubber gloves – you do not want to dye your hands as well.

Face-mask

Some of the chemicals used in the dyeing process may give off fumes, and finely powdered mordants, assistants and dyestuffs may be irritant, so wear a face-mask to avoid inhaling them, especially if you are asthmatic.

Safety notes

- Always follow the instructions supplied with any chemicals and dyestuffs you buy.
- Store all dyes, mordants and assistants in clearly labelled containers and keep them away from children, pets and food.
- Do not eat, drink or smoke while using these products.
- Keep pans solely for mordanting and dyeing and never use the same pans for food preparation. Cover the pans when in use to reduce fumes.
- Some dyestuffs and mordants are poisonous and irritant, so handle all of them with great care.
- All fine powders, whether toxic or not, are potentially harmful if inhaled.
- Some mordants give off toxic vapours if boiled. Never exceed simmering point (88°C/190°F max.) when mordanting. Always work in a well-ventilated area.
- Always wear rubber gloves and a face mask when using mordants and assistants and avoid contact with the skin and eyes.
- Seek medical advice if any substances come into contact with the eyes.
- Take particular care with the following chemical substances:
    Copper – poison.
    Tannic acid – harmful by inhalation and skin contact; irritant.
    Thiox – harmful; keep dry. Do not add water to *Thiox*; always add *Thiox* slowly to plenty of hot water.
    Dilute acids – handle with care.
- Never empty mordant baths down the sink; follow the instructions given below.

Environmental notes

All spent mordant baths should be disposed of down a foul drain (the lavatory), not the sink, together with plenty of clean water. This avoids splashes in areas where food is prepared. Used dyebaths or mordant baths containing small residues of alum, copper, iron or tannin may also be poured on the ground, but well away from septic tanks, wells, pets, or where children play. All these substances are either abundant in nature or used by gardeners.

The simple things you will need for your first dyeing project.

Dyeing a skein of yarn

The instructions here apply to wool and other animal (protein) fibres. When dyeing cotton and other vegetable (cellulose) fibres, you will need to make slight amendments to the procedure, and these are described later in this chapter (see page 24).

Note that if you are dyeing silk yarn or fabric, excessive heat may destroy its lustre: keep the temperature of the water in both the mordant pan and the dyebath below the simmering point of 82°C (180°F).

You will need

- 100g of natural woollen yarn
- 30g onion skins (the dyestuff). Use only the dry, brown outer skins (your local greengrocer might be a helpful contact)
- 8g alum (the mordant). This is sometimes available from good chemists
- 7g cream of tartar (the assistant)
- Some liquid detergent (the scouring agent)
- A water supply (see also page 11)

If you wish to dye a larger quantity of wool, increase all the above amounts proportionally.

Preparation

Skeins of wool must be tied in about four places to prevent tangling. Remember to use loose ties or you may end up with a tie-dye effect!

Make a note of the dry weight of the wool to be dyed. Preparing the yarn involves wetting it and it can be extremely annoying to have to dry the materials again if you forget.

All recipes in this book refer to quantities of mordants and dye-stuffs relative to the dry weight of the material to be dyed, and usually as percentages. For example, 30 per cent dyestuff means that you will need 30g of dyestuff for every 100g dry weight of material to be dyed.

Weighing the tied wool.

Scouring the wool

This means getting the wool completely clean. Any grease or dirt left on the material will result in patchy colours. The yarn must also be thoroughly wetted before you start the mordanting process.

Scour the yarn by soaking it overnight in a liquid-detergent solution (if it is very greasy it may need several scourings). Rinse it well and then gently squeeze out the excess water.

Sudden changes in the temperature of the liquid will cause woollen materials to mat or felt, so use cool or lukewarm water for scouring. When the water needs to be boiled, as in the following mordanting and dyeing processes, apply heat gradually to increase the temperature very slowly.

Scouring the wool.

Preparing the dyebath

Place the onion skins in the dyepan and cover them with water. If you are impatient you could pour boiling water on to the skins.

Then put the dyebath on to the heat source and slowly raise the temperature to boiling point. Reduce the heat and simmer for about forty-five minutes. At the end of this period, all the colour should have been extracted from the onion skins. Take the pan off the heat and allow to cool before straining off the onion skins.

Simmering onion skins to extract the colour.

Preparing the mordant bath

For this exercise, we will use alum and cream of tartar as the mordant and assistant. There are other mordant recipes for wool that will produce different shades of colour and degrees of fastness and these are discussed in the chapter on mordants (see page 24).

Dissolve the alum and cream of tartar in a little hot water and then add this solution to cool water in the mordant pan. Immerse the wetted yarn and then place the pan on the heat source. Slowly raise the temperature to 82°C (180°F) and simmer for forty-five minutes. Leave to cool, then remove the wool and rinse it well.

Mordanting the wool.

The dyeing process

When the dyebath is cool, add enough water to allow free movement of the batch of wool. Place the pre-mordanted, thoroughly wetted skein into the dyebath.

Put the dyebath back on to the heat and slowly raise the temperature to boiling point. Immediately reduce the heat and simmer at a temperature of 82°C (180°F) for thirty to forty-five minutes or until the wool is the colour you want it. Remember that wool will appear darker in colour when wet than when dry. If you want to prevent any further take-up of colour, remove the wool from the dyebath and allow it to cool in another container. Otherwise, turn off the heat and leave the dyebath and wool to cool together. Do not immerse the hot wool in cold water, as this can cause felting.

Simmering the wool in the dyebath until it is the colour you want.

Rinsing and drying

When the skein of wool is cool, rinse it thoroughly in several changes of water until the rinsing water is clear.

When all the excess dye has been rinsed away, wash the skein of wool in warm soapy water. Rinse again and allow to dry.

Allow the rinsed wool to dry.

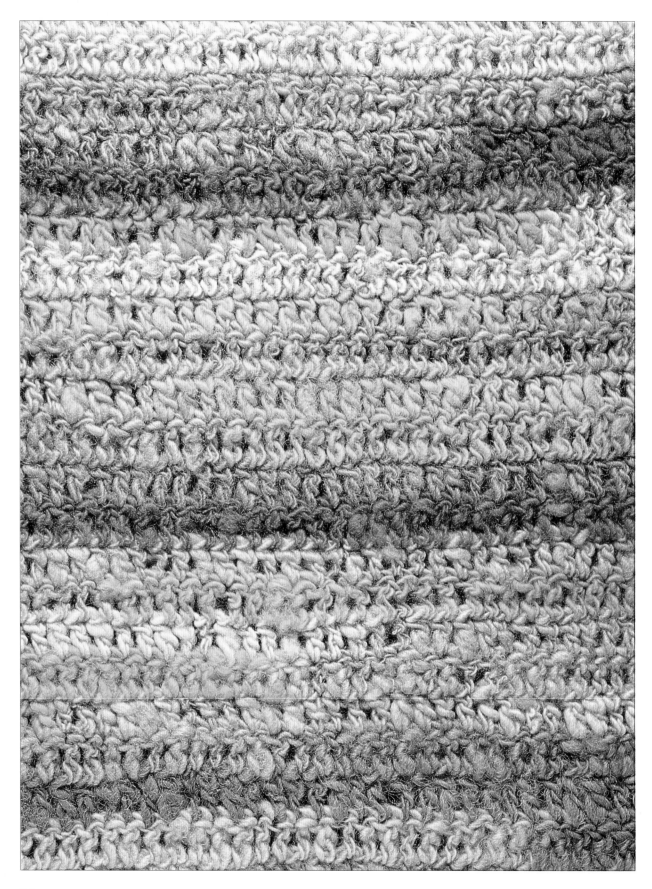

Dyeing cotton

Cotton and other vegetable fibres are generally less sensitive than wool, so they do not need to be treated with quite so much care.

To get the same degree of colour on cotton as on wool, you may need to use more dyestuff.

Mordants for cotton

Alum (with washing soda as an assistant) is by far the most common mordant used with cotton and other vegetable fibres. You will need 25g of alum and 6g of washing soda for each 100g dry weight of materials.

You will also need some more washing soda for the scouring of the material.

Scouring

Cotton and other vegetable fibres are less sensitive than wool and can be scoured by boiling in plenty of water. Add a handful of washing soda and a small amount of liquid detergent to a pan of water, immerse the cotton and then boil for about forty-five minutes. Rinse well before mordanting.

Preparing the mordant bath

Fill the mordanting pan two-thirds full with hot water and dissolve the alum, stirring well. Dissolve the washing soda in a little hot water and slowly add this solution to the pan. Top up with cold water. Some bubbles may appear; these are carbon dioxide gas being released.

When all the bubbles have subsided, add the wetted cotton yarn or fabric to the mordant bath and slowly raise the temperature to the simmering point of 82–88°C (180–190°F). Now turn off the heat and leave the cotton to steep overnight. Rinse well before dyeing.

The dyeing process

Dye the cotton as described for wool. As with wool, other mordant recipes can be used with onion skins: you will find these in the chapter on mordants (see page 24).

Opposite: Some of the beautiful shades produced by dyeing with onion skins.

Cotton yarn and fabric dyed with onion skins – the longer you simmer the yarn or fabric, the more intense the colour produced.

Keeping records

It is a good idea to get into the habit of keeping detailed records of the mordants and the precise quantities of dyestuffs used. Remember to make a note of any additions to the dyebath, such as citric acid or iron.

Finally, label your samples of dyed yarns and fabric with the details mentioned above.

Overleaf: Pages from my record book.

Madder

Wool
Alum 8%
C of T 7%

Mohair
loop
Copper 1%

Wool/synth.
Iron 7%

Grey fleece
Alum 8%

Silk
Alum 8%

Cotton
Alum/soda

Wool
Copper

Mohair
Iron

Linen
Alum

Wool/cotton
Alum

Grey wool
Alum

Tea

Wool
Alum +
C of T

Grey wool
Alum

Wool-bouclé
Copper

Mohair
Iron

Silk
Alum

Cotton
Alum

Linen
Alum

Wool/cotton
Alum

Turmeric

Cotton
Alum

Grey wool
Alum

Wool/cotton
Alum

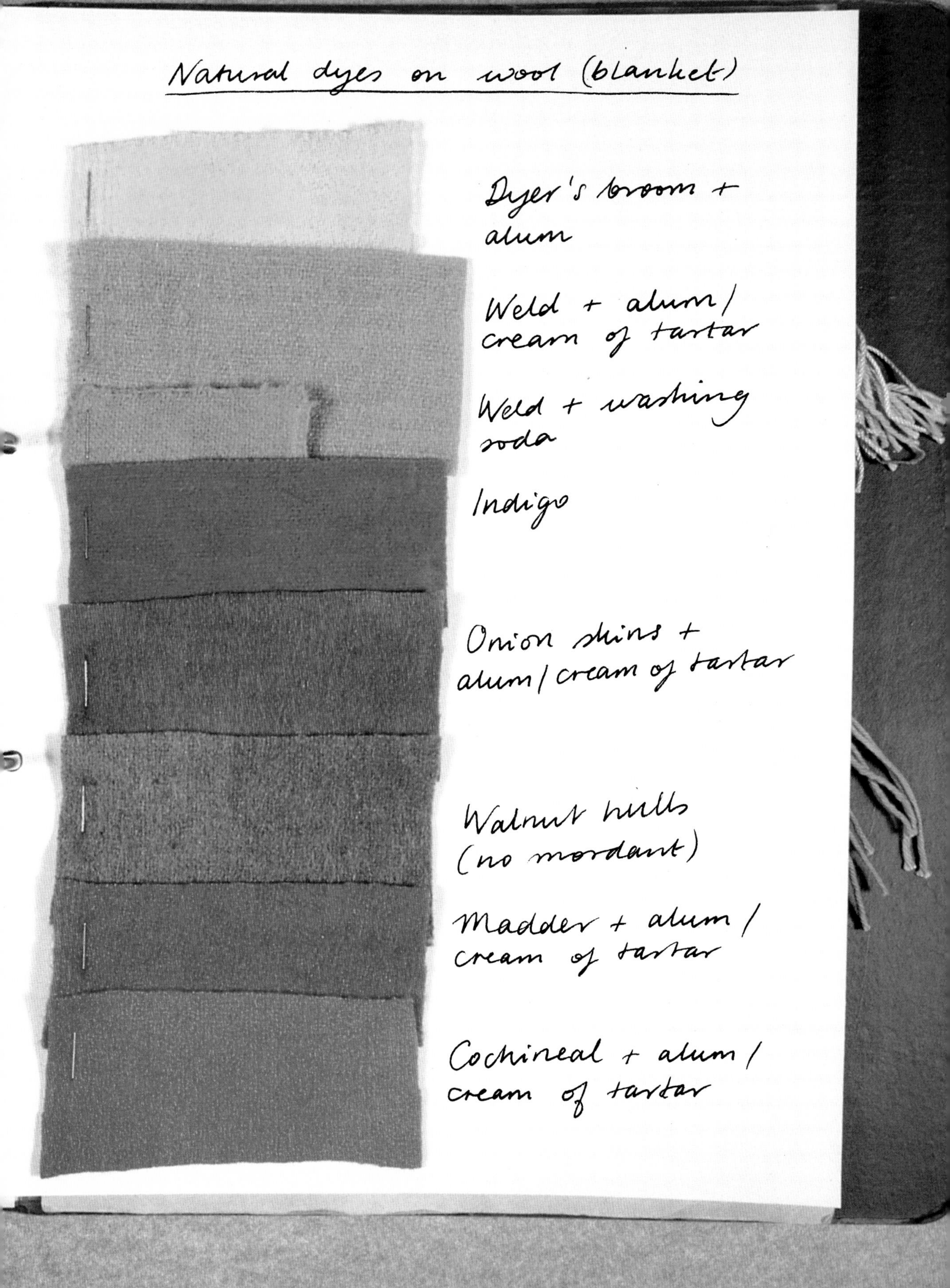

Natural dyes on wool (blanket)

Dyer's broom +
alum

Weld + alum /
cream of tartar

Weld + washing
soda

Indigo

Onion skins +
alum / cream of tartar

Walnut hulls
(no mordant)

Madder + alum /
cream of tartar

Cochineal + alum /
cream of tartar

Mordants

Mordants are substances that are used to fix a dye to the fibres. They fix a dye permanently to the fibres, improve the take-up of the dye colour, and enhance light- and wash-fastness. They are used in solution, often with the addition of an 'assistant' which improves the fixing of the mordant to the yarn or fibre.

Some dyestuffs will fix without the use of a mordant, and these are known as 'substantive' dyes. Some dyes, apart from substantive ones, can also be used without a mordant, but the resultant colours may be less light- and wash-fast. These include dyestuffs such as madder, weld, fustic, barberry bark and cutch. If you wish to improve the final colour characteristics, but are concerned about using chemical mordants, use a natural mordant.

In the distant past, most mordants would have come from natural sources, such as rock alum, iron-rich mud and naturally occurring mineral deposits. Where an alkali was needed, stale urine or wood-ash, from a wood fire, would have been used. Acids would have been obtained from acidic fruits, such as lemons and limes, or from other plant sources, such as rhubarb leaves, which contain oxalic acid. Nowadays, the natural dyer may need to use chemical

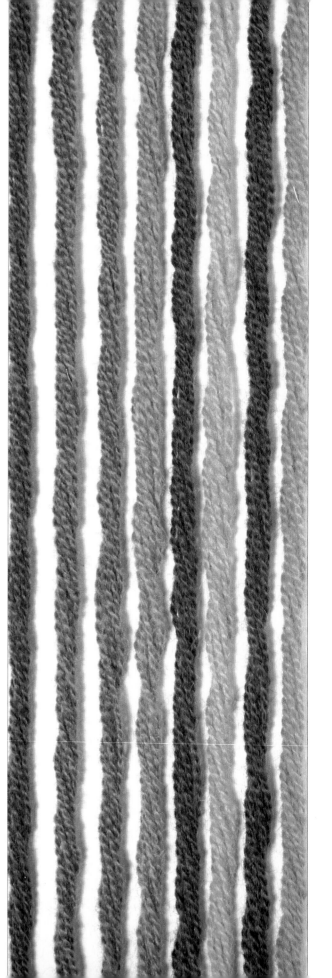

Substantive dyes (100 per cent dyestuff): from left to right

Alkanet used with iron as a colour modifier.
Alkanet used alone.
Walnut hulls used with iron as a colour modifier.
Walnut hulls used alone.
Rhubarb root used with iron as a colour modifier.
Rhubarb root used alone.
Henna used with iron as a colour modifier.
Henna used alone.

Natural mordants: sumach leaves, rhubarb leaves, white vinegar, lemon juice, iron water made with rusty nails, and oak galls.

mordants, such as alum, which can sometimes be obtained from chemists, although you may have to ask the chemist to order it for you. Cream of tartar, which is used with alum, can be bought from most supermarkets.

You will probably have to buy copper sulphate from specialist suppliers, but you can substitute white vinegar for the dilute acetic acid used with copper. Naturally occurring plant tannins, for example those found in oak galls and sumach leaves, can be used instead of tannic acid in cotton mordanting. You can use small amounts of washing soda to make liquids more alkaline, while vinegar or lemon juice, used in very small quantities, will make liquids more acidic.

Chrome is sometimes recommended as a mordant, but because of its highly toxic nature and potential for environmental pollution it has not been included in this book. It was not one of the naturally occurring substances used in the past and was not used as a mordant for natural dyeing until the mid nineteenth century. Many of the shades obtained from a chrome mordant can be obtained in other ways, either by using a different dyestuff, or by using copper as a mordant or iron as a colour modifier.

Natural mordants

There are a few plants – club mosses and tea leaves for example – which contain aluminium in small quantities. These may well be considered as alternatives to alum, for mordanting both wool and cotton materials. However, in practice, it is difficult to know how much aluminium there is in each plant. In addition, club mosses are rare, so unless you have your own sustainable source, it may be better to use alum and cream of tartar for wool mordanting.

Iron water may be used as an alternative to ferrous sulphate, either as a mordant or as a modifier (after-mordant). Iron water can be made quite easily by adding a few rusty nails to an iron or plastic bucket of water mixed with a cupful of vinegar. Leave them for a week or two until the water looks rusty. Use as required and then add more water to keep it topped up.

Oak galls or sumach leaves make a good alternative to tannic acid for cotton mordanting (see page 30). Rhubarb leaves contain oxalic acid and can often be used on wool and silk as a base for other dyes. Simmer the leaves gently in a covered pan for about an hour, using 50 per cent to 100 per cent leaves to the dry weight of wool. Strain off the liquid into the mordanting pan and simmer the wool or silk in the bath for forty-five minutes. This will give the yarn or fabric a pale yellow/green colour and will affect the shades produced in subsequent dyebaths. It is also a fairly fast dye in its own right.

Note Oxalic acid is poisonous, so keep the pans covered and do not breathe in any fumes.

Always handle mordants with care. Wear rubber gloves, cover the pans and work in a well-ventilated area.

Chemical mordants

Chemical mordants are metallic salts. If you have any worries about using chemical mordants, some of which are toxic, keep to the substantive dyes or use natural plant alternatives.

The most common chemical mordants are alum and copper for wool, and alum and tannic acid for cotton. Of these, alum is the simplest mordant to choose as it is sometimes available from good chemists; more importantly, and unlike copper, it is not poisonous.

The type of mordant used will affect the colour produced by the dyestuff, so a variety of shades can be produced from a single dyebath by treating individual skeins of yarn with different mordants.

The degree of light-fastness of some dyestuffs may also be influenced by the choice of mordant.

Alum, with cream of tartar as an assistant, is the safest mordant, both for the user and for the environment. If you use alum alone, or with washing soda (for cotton) there will be a little alum left in the spent mordant bath: this must be disposed of carefully (see page 15).

Iron and tannin are abundant in nature and the small quantities used by natural dyers will present no threat to the environment if the spent mordant bath is disposed of correctly.

If you use copper, always use it with dilute acetic acid (or white vinegar), and always in the way I describe. By following these instructions there will be virtually no copper left in the spent mordant bath, which can then be disposed of safely, as described on page 15.

Tin and chrome, two other recognised chemical mordants, should be avoided because of their potential for environmental pollution.

Making mordant solutions

Very small amounts of chemical mordants are required, so if you do not have a set of scales that

Undyed wool mordanted with a rhubarb solution.

Undyed wool mordanted with copper.

Madder on wool mordanted with iron.

Madder on wool mordanted with copper.

Madder on wool mordanted with alum.

Cochineal on wool mordanted with iron.

Cochineal on wool mordanted with copper.

Cochineal on wool mordanted with alum.

Weld on wool mordanted with iron.

Weld on wool mordanted with copper.

Weld on wool mordanted with alum.

can measure these precisely you will find it easier to make them into a stock solution. I use metric measurements: see page 14 for guidance on imperial measurements.

Dissolve the mordant powder in hot water at a ratio of 1g of mordant to 10ml of water. This means that 50g of mordant will make 500ml of solution and 100g will make 1 litre of solution. Store the solution (clearly labelled) in a dark bottle. Mordants made in this way will keep indefinitely. When you need 1g of mordant, syringe out 10ml of solution (80ml for 8g).

From a safety point of view, making a mordant solution is a good idea as it avoids frequently working with fine powders. Any spillage of dilute mordant liquids is easier and safer to mop up than spilt powder; mop it up with paper towels which can then be shredded and flushed down the lavatory. Before disposing of spilt powders in the same way, dilute them with plenty of water.

Quantities to use

In the past most craft dyers have used larger quantities of mordants than are now considered necessary or desirable.

Recent research shows that using smaller quantities of mordants together with assistants gives more reliable results and ensures that there is little or no mordant residue returned to the environment when the spent mordant bath is disposed of.

Mordanting animal fibres

There are two basic mordants that can be used with animal fibres: alum with cream of tartar; and copper with acetic acid. Of the two, alum is the safer mordant, but, if prepared and used correctly, copper can provide a wider range of colours and sometimes better light-fastness.

Note In the following recipes the mordant solution is raised to a simmering temperature of 82°C (180°F). When silk yarn or fabric is to be mordanted, the temperature in the mordant bath must be kept below 82°C (180°F) because excessive heat may destroy the lustre of the silk.

Alum and cream of tartar

This recipe was used in the exercise to dye a skein of yarn and is described on page 18.

Copper and acetic acid

When used with acetic acid, smaller quantities of copper can be used, and the use of acetic acid greatly improves the take-up of copper by the material being mordanted, leaving hardly any residue in the spent mordant bath.

Proportions
2g copper and 40ml of 5 per cent dilute acetic acid (or white vinegar) per 100g wool.

Method
Dissolve the copper in hot water and add it to the cool mordant bath. Add the dilute acetic acid and stir well. Add the yarn and slowly raise the temperature to 82°C (180°F). Simmer for forty-five minutes, leave to cool, and rinse well.

Iron (ferrous sulphate) as a colour modifier

Method
Dye your yarn or fabric with your chosen mordant, or without a mordant, and then remove the dyed material from the dyebath, add 2 per cent iron (*i.e.* 2g iron per 100g dry weight of yarn or fabric) to the used dyebath, and stir well. Then return the dyed material to the dyebath, simmer for five minutes, leave to cool and rinse well.

Mordanting vegetable fibres

Alum (with washing soda as an assistant) is by far the most common mordant used with cotton and other vegetable fibres, although tannin, in the form of tannic acid, oak galls or sumach leaves, can also be used.

I have included three recipes that I use: one for alum with washing soda; one for tannin, in all its forms; and a third, a three-step process, that is known as the alum/tannin/alum method. The third recipe does take longer, but the results are so much better than with the other two.

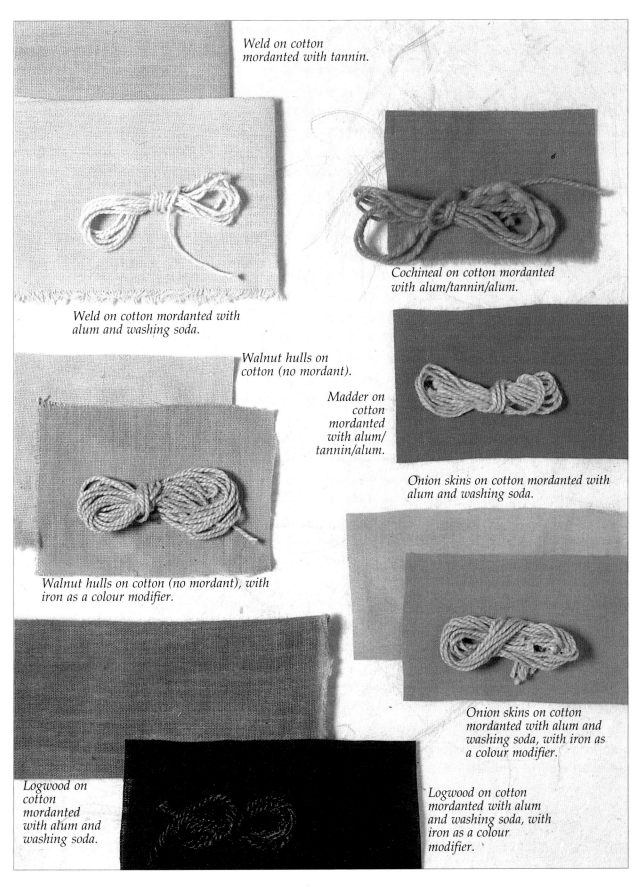

Weld on cotton mordanted with tannin.

Cochineal on cotton mordanted with alum/tannin/alum.

Weld on cotton mordanted with alum and washing soda.

Walnut hulls on cotton (no mordant).

Madder on cotton mordanted with alum/ tannin/alum.

Onion skins on cotton mordanted with alum and washing soda.

Walnut hulls on cotton (no mordant), with iron as a colour modifier.

Onion skins on cotton mordanted with alum and washing soda, with iron as a colour modifier.

Logwood on cotton mordanted with alum and washing soda.

Logwood on cotton mordanted with alum and washing soda, with iron as a colour modifier.

Alum with washing soda

We used this recipe in dyeing a skein of yarn, and it is described on page 21.

Tannin

Tannin is available as tannic acid, or it can be obtained from oak galls or sumach leaves. Used alone, tannin does not produce good colours with all dyestuffs, but it does work with onion skins, cutch, walnut hulls and fustic.

Tannin will leave the yarn or fabric a beige colour, so if you intend to tie-dye and want a white background, you will need to bind the areas that are to remain white before beginning the mordanting process.

Proportions
Tannin – 6g tannic acid, 60g oak galls or 50g fresh (25g dried) sumach leaves per 100g cotton.

Method
If using tannic acid, fill the mordanting pan half-full with hot water and add the acid, stirring well to make sure that it has dissolved completely. Top up with cold water.

I have occasionally had problems with tannic acid. I have found that some particles stick to the bottom of the mordanting pan or the material. This may cause staining which can result in patchy dyeing. To avoid this, do make sure that the acid is fully dissolved and move the yarn or fabric gently in the mordant bath from time to time.

Both oak galls and sumach leaves, whichever you have chosen to use, should be soaked in cold water overnight. Then bring them to boiling point and simmer them for an hour to extract the tannin. When the liquid is cool, strain it into the mordanting pan and then top up with enough water to allow the material to move freely.

When the mordant is ready to use, add the wetted cotton. Slowly raise the temperature to the simmering point of 82–88°C (180–190°F), turn off the heat and leave to steep overnight.

Rinse well before dyeing.

Three-step alum/tannin/alum

This method does take longer than the others, but it gives much better results. Quite simply, it involves mordanting the cotton three times. The first time use the alum with washing soda recipe. Next, mordant the yarn or fabric with one of the tannin recipes. Finally, use the alum with washing soda recipe again.

After-mordants for cotton

The colours produced from tannin-mordanted cotton and other vegetable fibres can be enhanced by applying an after-mordant immediately after dyeing.

Proportions
Two chemicals can be used as after-mordants: copper (with acetic acid) and iron.

COPPER: 2g copper and 40ml of 5 per cent dilute acetic acid or white vinegar per 100g cotton.

IRON: Use 2g of ferrous sulphate per 100g cotton.

Method
The following method applies to both the after-mordants mentioned above.

Add the after-mordant chemicals to a pan of hot water, stirring well to ensure an even solution. Immerse the dyed cotton in the liquid and raise the temperature to the simmering point. Simmer very gently for ten minutes, remove the cotton and rinse well.

Dyestuffs

In this chapter I give broad outlines of where to look for potential sources of colour. While virtually any organic material will produce some colour in the dyebath and may also give some shade on yarn or fabric, such colours are often fugitive – the colour soon fades away. I have included many suggestions, but I would only really recommend the use of plants which have stood the test of time and proved themselves reliable as dyestuffs.

However, for the craft dyer whose main aim is experimentation and who is prepared to accept virtually any shade or hue, however fugitive, the possibilities are almost infinite.

From very early times, as long as 5,000 years ago, madder and indigo were in use in many parts of the world. Considerably later, the discovery of the Americas led to the wider use of the other great natural dyes such as logwood, fustic and cochineal. All these dyes are still grown commercially, either as dyestuffs or for other purposes, and can be obtained from specialist dyestuff suppliers. Yellow-producing dyestuffs have always been abundant all over the world and in each country there would be many sources of yellow, which is the most common colour produced from plants.

Natural dyestuffs fall mainly into the following broad categories: leaves and stems; twigs and tree prunings; flower heads; barks; roots; insect dyes; outer skins, hulls and husks; heartwoods and wood-shavings; berries and seeds; and lichens.

You should never uproot any plant that you find growing in the wild. Many species are protected, so this may be against the law anyway.

Some leaves and berries can be collected without damaging the plant or tree, but do not pick *all* the berries, as they contain the seeds for future plants.

Roots and bark of living plants should always be left alone, as plants can be fatally damaged if bark is stripped off or if the roots are disturbed.

Do not gather lichens from the wild as these are generally classed as protected organisms and very often take many years to grow. You may be able to get some lichens at woodyards or saw mills, from felled trees awaiting processing, but always ask permission first. However, even lichens growing on felled trees continue to live for many years, so make sure you only collect those which would otherwise be removed and destroyed.

Quantities required

As a general rule of thumb, the ratio of dyestuff to material to be dyed is 100 per cent: *i.e.* to dye 50g of wool you will need 50g of dyestuff.

However, there are some exceptions:

- Cochineal – 20 per cent
- Fustic – 50 per cent
- Logwood – 10 to 50 per cent
- Persian berries – 30 per cent
- Turmeric – 50 per cent

Using more dyestuff will result in darker shades; using less will result in paler shades. The paler shades may be less light-fast.

Testing dye potential

Testing dyestuffs is a pleasant and rewarding occupation in itself, so always take every opportunity to test the plants growing around you (provided that they are in your garden and not in the wild).

It is always useful to test dyestuffs on samples of yarn pre-mordanted with different mordants, but make sure you know which is which!

To test a plant for its dye potential, you should follow the general instructions given in this chapter for the part of the plant you wish to test.

Privet.

Cow parsley.

Nettles.

Carrot tops.

Goldenrod.

Eucalyptus.

Woad.

Bracken.

Birch.

Ivy.

Leaves and stems

Many freshly gathered young leaves and stems yield some sort of yellow-green colour; for example weld, nettles, cow parsley, carrot, bracken, privet, ivy, goldenrod, birch, dyer's broom and eucalyptus.

Sometimes cold soaking of fresh leaves in a warm sunny place for several days, together with the yarn or cloth, will produce brighter shades than boiling, but, in general, leaves are boiled until they give off their colour and the resultant liquid is strained off and used as the dyebath. However, it is difficult to know in advance exactly which shade of yellowy-green each plant will produce in any one dyebath.

The blue-yielding dyestuffs indigo and woad are also produced from the leaves of plants. They are used rather differently from most other dyestuffs (see pages 44–48).

Twigs and tree prunings

Cut these into small pieces, soak them in cold water for several weeks, then boil them to extract the colour. Generally they produce beige and light-brown to pinky shades.

Flower heads

These should be gathered in full bloom. They generally give yellows to rusts, irrespective of the colour the flower itself may have been. Dahlias give good yellows and rusts; goldenrod, tansy, marigold, coreopsis and chamomile give various shades of yellow.

Only the flower heads are used, and frequently you do need a considerable quantity to produce good strong colours – often as much as 200 per cent.

Some flower heads can be used without boiling: soak the pre-mordanted yarn in a glass jar of cold water, together with the flower heads, over a period of several days, preferably in a warm sunny spot. Dahlias give good results by this method. If you boil the flower heads to extract the colour, do not boil too fiercely, as excess heat may destroy some of the colour. A slow simmer is best. You can also put the flower heads in a muslin bag and add the pre-mordanted yarn during the process of dye extraction, rather than straining off the dye liquid and then adding the yarn. You can also dry flower heads to use later.

Safflower petals are unusual in that they produce a shocking pink on cotton and silk if used according to the instructions on page 51.

Goldenrod.

Tansy.

Coreopsis.

Marigolds.

Chamomile.

Dahlias.

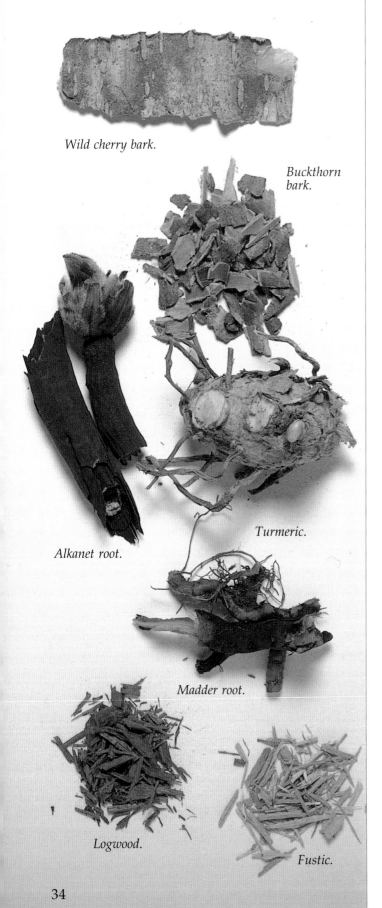

Wild cherry bark.

Buckthorn bark.

Alkanet root.

Turmeric.

Madder root.

Logwood.

Fustic.

Barks

Like twigs and tree prunings, barks need prior soaking – often for several days or even weeks. In general, they give mainly beige/tan shades. I have had good results with wild cherry bark and buckthorn bark.

Similar colours are often available from other sources. For experimental purposes, you could try out bark taken from fallen or pruned branches, but do not expect any particularly exciting results!

Roots

A small number of well-known dyestuffs come from roots. These include madder (reds and corals), turmeric (yellow), the substantive dye alkanet (greys and lavenders), and butternut-root bark (browns).

Madder is a very valuable dye-plant which can be grown quite easily in the garden – details of how to grow and use this dyestuff are given on pages 58–59 and 52–53 respectively. Otherwise, unless grown specifically for dyeing, roots should be left undisturbed.

Heartwoods and wood-shavings

Several valuable dyestuffs are heartwoods. These include fustic (yellows), logwood (purples, greys and black), and cutch (browns).

All these are of foreign origin and can be bought, usually in the form of chips or powder, from dyestuff suppliers.

Some wood shavings give useful yellows, pinks and browns, and there is scope for experimentation here, especially if you have a woodworker in the family. Do not use wood-dust, though, as it is harmful if inhaled.

Yew shavings (yellows and rusts) are worth trying, but remember that yew is poisonous.

Outer skins, hulls and husks

Onion skins are a useful dyestuff and I always save bags full for dyeing purposes. Only the outer brown (or sometimes red) skins are used and the colours produced range from yellows to rusts and browns.

Black walnut hulls give good shades of brown and can be used without a mordant. With the addition of iron as a modifier, they often give almost black shades.

Berries and seeds

Very few berries and seeds give reliable, worthwhile colours. The exceptions are annatto seeds for shades of orange, juniper berries for olive browns, and Persian berries (the dried berries of the buckthorn) for yellows.

Elderberries are popular with some hobby dyers, probably because they are so freely available and initially give bright pinky-purples. They are not really reliable, though, since the colours fade rapidly or change to brown or green.

If you do want to use berries, crush them before boiling them.

Lichens

Most lichens produce shades of yellow, rust and brown, and occasionally olive green on wool. Some give pinks and purples when fermented first in a solution of two parts water to one part household ammonia.

Lichens are substantive dyes which can be used without a mordant. Better colours are usually achieved if the lichen is left in the dyebath during dyeing and very gently simmered for several hours. However, I have found that lichens do not produce very strong, fast colours on cotton yarn or cloth.

Onion skins.

Buckthorn berries.

Juniper berries.

Elderberries.

Lichen.

Insect dyes

Certain insects from other countries produce valuable red and pink dyes – for example cochineal. You can buy them in dried form from dyestuff suppliers and although they are generally quite expensive, a little goes a long way.

Cochineal beetles.

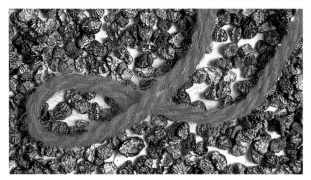

Extracting the dye colour

There are two basic methods of extracting the colour from dyestuffs. Natural dyestuffs in the form of petals, leaves, stems, etc., require boiling. Exceptions are safflower, woad, indigo and madder, all of which are discussed where they occur. Dyestuffs in powder or extract form need only be mixed with water.

Boiling

To extract the dye colour, put the dyestuff in a pan, fill the pan with water, bring it to the boil and then simmer for forty-five minutes to an hour. Strain off the liquid into the dyepan and leave to cool before adding the yarn.

It may be possible to boil up the dyestuff again to extract more colour for a second dyebath, but this will depend on the type of dyestuff.

Mixing powders and extracts

Some dyestuffs (*e.g.* cutch and henna) are supplied in powder form. Mix the powder to a paste with some cold water, then gradually add more water, stirring all the time, until you have enough for your dyebath. Add the yarn or fabric and dye according to the usual method. The dyed material will need to be thoroughly rinsed and washed to remove all traces of powder particles.

Dye extracts, such as logwood extract, will dissolve completely in hot water and can simply be stirred into the dyebath. Remember that extracts are much stronger than dye chips, so you will need to use only about one-fifth to one-quarter of the quantities given for chips.

Testing for light-fastness

Once you have dyed your samples, you should test them for light-fastness by sandwiching the samples between sheets of card, leaving a portion of each protruding from the edge. Place the samples in a sunny window for several weeks and then check the colours on the exposed edges against those of the covered parts.

This method sounds a bit unscientific, but it will give you an idea of the extent to which the colours are likely to fade.

To get a clearer idea as to how to interpret the degree of colour change on the exposed edges, it is useful to add a sample with a known degree of light-fastness to the samples you are testing and to use this as a 'control'. For example, alum-mordanted wool dyed with madder has good fastness to light and if a sample is tested at the same time as your other samples, then you would be able to draw these conclusions from your tests: any samples which fade before the madder sample are less light-fast (*i.e.* not so good), while those which show fading at the same time as the madder sample can be considered to have good fastness to light.

As a basic rule of thumb, dyestuffs with a good light-fastness are suitable for all uses, including tapestries and furnishings which are regularly exposed to daylight. Dyestuffs with a moderate light-fastness are less suitable for items which may be exposed to regular daylight, but are quite suitable for clothing. Those dyestuffs with only limited light-fastness are not really suitable for items such as tapestries and furnishings, but are quite adequate for clothing which is worn for a brief period and then stored in a dark place.

Testing for light-fastness. After exposing your samples to light, fold back the card and check the colours on the exposed edges against those of the covered parts.

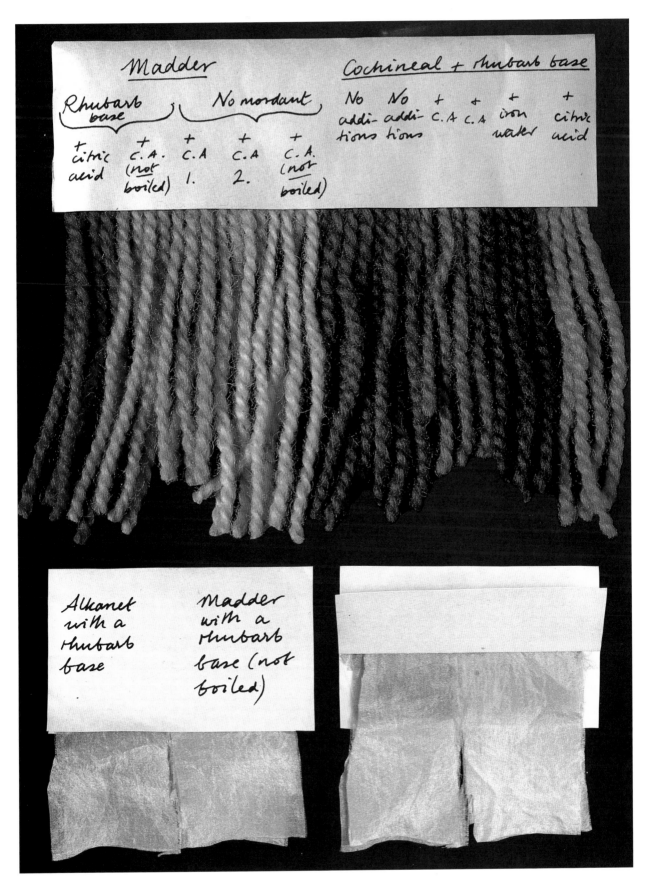

Madder

Cochineal + rhubarb base

Rhubarb base

No mordant

No additions No additions + C.A + C.A + iron water + citric acid

+ citric acid + C.A. (not boiled) + C.A 1. + C.A 2. + C.A. (not boiled)

Alkanet with a rhubarb base

Madder with a rhubarb base (not boiled)

Cochineal on cotton over-dyed with indigo – dip 1.

Cochineal on cotton over-dyed with indigo – dip 2.

Cochineal on cotton over-dyed with indigo – dip 3.

Over-dyed wool.

Weld on cotton over-dyed with indigo.

Iron water with washing soda afterbath on cotton, over-dyed with indigo.

Dye mixing

It is possible to boil two or more dyestuffs together (except indigo) to make a dyebath that will produce a particular colour or shade. Use the same methods of colour extraction as given earlier.

Colour mixing of dyestuffs follows the basic principles of mixing colours used in other art forms and there is considerable scope for experimentation.

For example:
yellow + blue = green
pink + blue = purple
yellow + red = orange
red + blue + yellow = black

However, it is very difficult to assess just how much of each dye colour to use in dye mixing, and it is almost impossible to make colour adjustments as you proceed. Unless you have first experimented with percentages of each dyestuff, it is probably safer to use the method of over-dyeing given below.

Over-dyeing

Over-dyeing, which is also known as bottoming or top-dyeing, is my preferred method of creating colours that are unobtainable from single dyestuffs.

Basically, the method involves dyeing pre-mordanted yarn or cloth with the lightest shade of colour in the colour-mix recipe and then over-dyeing with successive colours. You can then remove the yarn or cloth from each dyebath when the required depth of colour is obtained.

I use this method mainly to produce greens by dipping yellow-dyed yarn in a vat of indigo, but it can also be used in combination with other dyestuffs to achieve colour variations.

Whichever way you approach colour mixing, you will need to experiment first with small samples. But it can be great fun!

Over-dyeing: the best way to get true greens.

A world of natural colour

In this chapter I attempt to give you some pointers towards getting the right colours, the fibre/mordant combinations that can be used, and an indication of the light-fastness.

Basically, the craft dyer needs reliable sources of yellows, reds, pinks, browns and blues. Virtually all other colours and shades can be achieved from a combination of two or more of these colours.

Although on the following pages I have listed a variety of dyestuffs that can give colours in particular parts of the spectrum, not all are light-fast. For the ones that I use most regularly I have included guidance on dyestuff/mordant combinations for both animal and vegetable fibres, together with an indication of how light-fast I have found each to be. The abbreviations G (for good), M (for moderate) and L (for limited) against each substance I have tested will give you an idea.

This is not an exhaustive list, so do not be put off trying out other dyestuffs.

Yellows and golds

The indications of the degree of light-fastness given in this section are to help you choose which dyestuff to use for your purpose (see page 36).

Weld *Reseda luteola*

Wool
MORDANT: copper (G).
MORDANT: alum (L).

Fustic *Morus tinctoria, Chlorophora tinctoria*

Use 50 per cent dyestuff for all fibres.

Wool
MORDANT: copper (G).
MORDANT: alum (M).

Cotton
MORDANT: alum/tannin/alum (M).
MORDANT: alum/washing soda (L).
MORDANT: tannin (M).

Persian berries (buckthorn) *Rhamnus* species

Use 10–25 per cent dyestuff.

Wool
MORDANT: alum (M).

Onion skins *Allium cepa*

Use 30 per cent dyestuff.

Wool
MORDANT: alum (L).

Cotton
MORDANT: use any of the three cotton mordanting recipes (L).

Nettles *Urtica dioica*

Use 200 per cent dyestuff. The shades produced by these mordants vary considerably from beiges to yellowy-greens.

Wool
MORDANT: alum (M).
MORDANT: copper (M).

Weld on wool.

Fustic on cotton.

Fustic on woollen fabric.

*Rhubarb
root on
silk.*

*Iron water with
washing-soda
afterbath on silk.*

Safflower on wool.

Onion skins on wool.

Iron

Iron, in the form of ferrous sulphate solution or iron water, can be used to produce light-fast shades of yellow and rust on cotton, linen or silk. Note that the following recipes are not suitable for use with wool.

Ferrous sulphate solution

Use one tablespoon per two litres or two level tablespoons of ferrous sulphate per gallon of water. Dissolve the ferrous sulphate in hot water, stirring well to make sure that it is completely dissolved. Add this solution to the rest of the water, again stirring well.

Iron water

Put some rusty nails or pieces of rusty iron in an iron pot (or plastic bucket). Fill the pot with water and add one or two cups of vinegar, preferably white vinegar or 5 per cent dilute acetic acid. Leave to steep for at least a week before use. To use, strain off the required amount of iron water and top up the pot with more water to ensure a continuous supply.

Now simmer the material in the iron solution for fifteen to thirty minutes. Alternatively, work the material in cold iron solution for fifteen to thirty minutes, moving it about frequently. Squeeze out excess moisture, do not rinse, and allow the colour to develop in the air.

If you are dyeing fabric, open it out immediately to prevent any rusty crease lines from developing. Repeat the process for deeper shades. Rinse, wash and then rinse again.

Safflower

Boiled safflower petals produce a yellow dye colour (less fast than that from fustic or weld) which is more suitable for wool and silk than for cotton. The yarn or cloth to be dyed must be mordanted first.

41

Other plants

There are a number of other sources of yellow, most (except for coreopsis) more suitable for use on wool than on cotton. Most have limited light-fastness, but nonetheless you can get some very pretty colours.

Cow parsley (*Anthriscus sylvestris*)
Dyer's broom (*Genista tinctoria*)
Tansy (*Tanacetum vulgare*)
Marigold (*Tagetes* and *Calendula* species)
Coreopsis (*Coreopsis tinctoria*)
Goldenrod (*Solidago canadensis*)
Chamomile (*Matricaria chamomila*)
Dyer's chamomile (*Anthemis tinctoria*) (improved light-fastness with a copper mordant)
Dahlia (*Dahlia* species)
Bracken (*Pteridium aquilinum*)
Birch (*Betula* species)
Eucalyptus (*Eucalyptus* species)
Ivy (*Hedera* species)
Privet leaves (*Ligustrum vulgare*)
Yew shavings (*Taxus* species)
Carrot tops (*Daucus carota*)
Turmeric roots (*Curcuma longa*)

Dahlia on wool mordanted with alum.

Turmeric on wool/cotton.

Dyer's broom on wool mordanted with alum.

Birch leaves on wool.

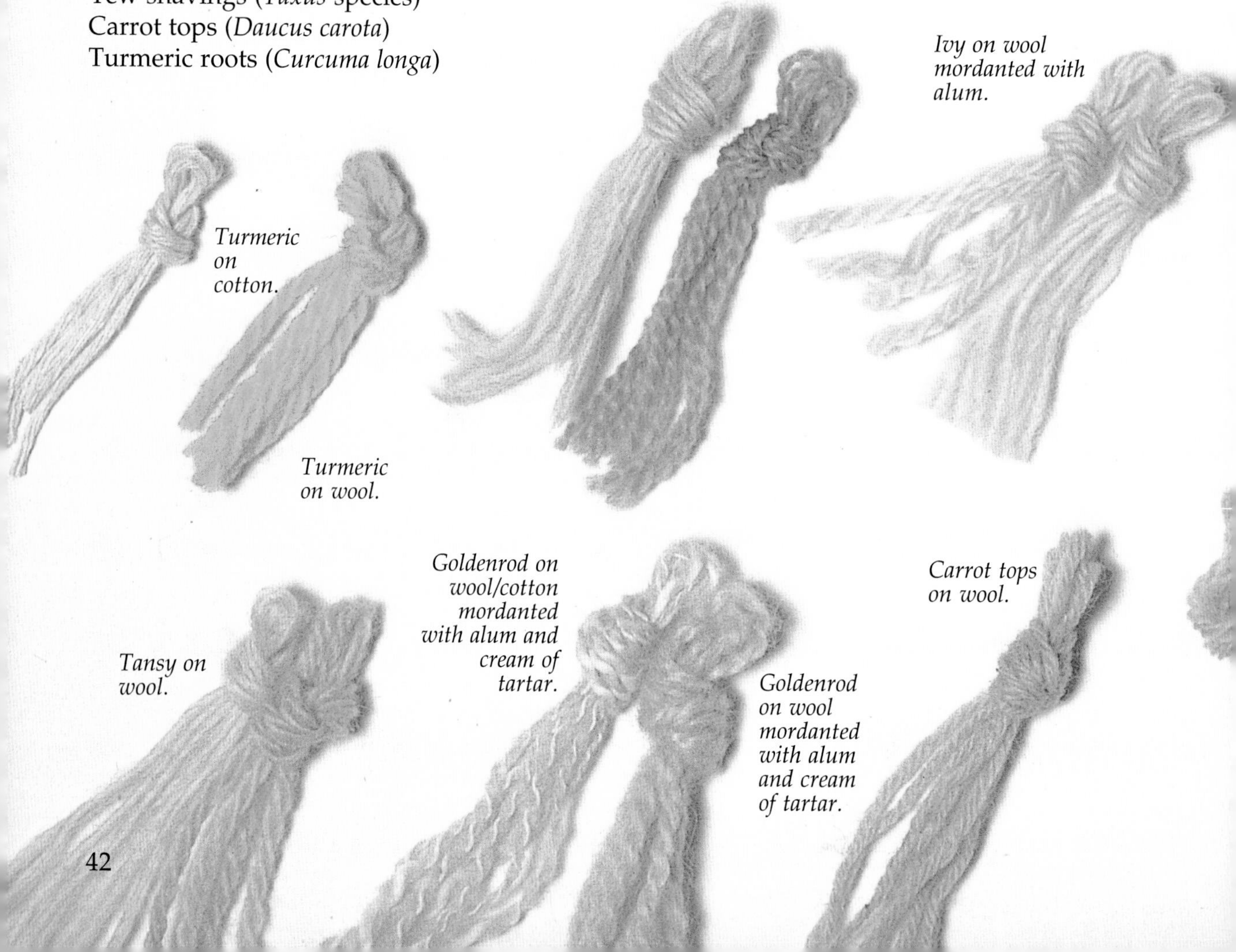

Ivy on wool mordanted with alum.

Turmeric on cotton.

Turmeric on wool.

Tansy on wool.

Goldenrod on wool/cotton mordanted with alum and cream of tartar.

Goldenrod on wool mordanted with alum and cream of tartar.

Carrot tops on wool.

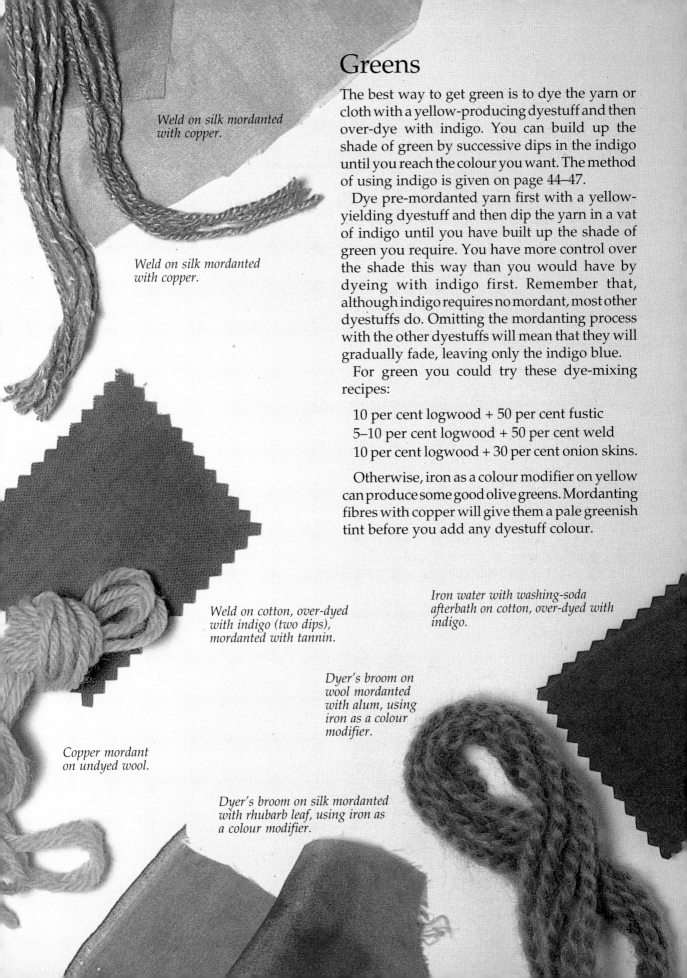

Greens

The best way to get green is to dye the yarn or cloth with a yellow-producing dyestuff and then over-dye with indigo. You can build up the shade of green by successive dips in the indigo until you reach the colour you want. The method of using indigo is given on page 44–47.

Dye pre-mordanted yarn first with a yellow-yielding dyestuff and then dip the yarn in a vat of indigo until you have built up the shade of green you require. You have more control over the shade this way than you would have by dyeing with indigo first. Remember that, although indigo requires no mordant, most other dyestuffs do. Omitting the mordanting process with the other dyestuffs will mean that they will gradually fade, leaving only the indigo blue.

For green you could try these dye-mixing recipes:

10 per cent logwood + 50 per cent fustic
5–10 per cent logwood + 50 per cent weld
10 per cent logwood + 30 per cent onion skins.

Otherwise, iron as a colour modifier on yellow can produce some good olive greens. Mordanting fibres with copper will give them a pale greenish tint before you add any dyestuff colour.

Weld on silk mordanted with copper.

Weld on silk mordanted with copper.

Weld on cotton, over-dyed with indigo (two dips), mordanted with tannin.

Iron water with washing-soda afterbath on cotton, over-dyed with indigo.

Dyer's broom on wool mordanted with alum, using iron as a colour modifier.

Copper mordant on undyed wool.

Dyer's broom on silk mordanted with rhubarb leaf, using iron as a colour modifier.

Blues

Indigo *Indigofera* species

Many people believe that indigo is a difficult dye to use and tend to avoid it. It is true that the preparation of the indigo vat needs care and accuracy, but once you have done that, indigo is one of the simplest and quickest of dyes to use. It is indispensable if you want to produce good, reliable, light-fast blues and greens.

Indigo is not native to Europe and grows mainly in Asia, Africa and South America. It is usually available in the form of a dark-blue powder, obtained from the leaves of various species of indigo plants.

You can also buy synthetic indigo, which is chemically the same as natural indigo. Synthetic indigo is also much stronger, so you need to use only half the quantity given for natural indigo.

Store indigo powder carefully, especially synthetic indigo (which can be sticky), because if spilt it is very difficult to remove from tiles, wood and carpets. It is best stored in a dark place, perhaps in a jar within a larger jar for safety.

Indigo is a substantive dye and therefore requires no mordant.

You can dye with it in a plastic bucket, as indigo does not require boiling, and indeed a cool vat is required for cotton. It can, however, be rather messy and I prefer to use indigo outside or in my outhouse, where drips do not matter. If you do use indigo in the kitchen, put plenty of newspaper on the floor and around your working area. Wear rubber gloves too, as indigo will colour your skin as well as your yarn or cloth!

How indigo works

Indigo in its blue state will not stick permanently to the material being dyed and must first be reduced to so-called 'indigo white'. This is achieved by combining it in a vat with an alkaline solution (a solution of washing soda) and a reducing agent (*Thiox* or sodium dithionite, or a colour-run-remover containing sodium hydrosulphite, such as *Beckmann's* or *RIT*), to remove all oxygen.

Indigo on silk.

Indigo on silk.

Indigo on wool.

Indigo on cotton – one dip.

Indigo on cotton – two dips.

Indigo on cotton – three dips.

Indigo on cotton yarn – four dips.

Indigo on wool.

Indigo on mohair loop – one dip.

In on w

44

*Indigo on
cotton yarn.*

*Indigo
on cotton
yarn.*

*Indigo on wool,
boiled in iron sol-
ution afterwards.*

It is very important not to introduce any oxygen (via air bubbles or drips of water, for example) to the vat during the dyeing process, as this will convert the 'indigo white' back to 'indigo blue' and greatly reduce the effectiveness of the vat, eventually making it useless. Exposure to the air makes the indigo return to its blue state when it is permanently fixed to the fibres.

Safety note

Do not add water to reducing agents – they generate heat when wetted and could catch fire. Add the reducing agent to the water slowly and carefully. *Thiox* and colour-run-remover are more stable than sodium dithionite/hydrosulphite, which must be handled with particular care. All reducing agents must be stored in a dry place. Wear rubber gloves when handling them as they are all harmful. It is wise to wear a face mask to avoid breathing in any particles or fumes when using these substances, particularly if you are asthmatic.

Please read all the following instructions carefully and understand all the implications before starting to use indigo.

Making a four-litre/one-gallon vat of indigo

The amount of material which can be dyed in a single vat will vary and is dependent on the depth of colour required and, to a very large extent, on the skill of the dyer in managing the vat.

Dissolve 50g washing soda in 30ml of boiling water and allow to cool slightly.

In a heatproof glass jug or jar, mix two teaspoons of natural indigo or one teaspoon of synthetic indigo into a paste with a little warm water (approximately two tablespoons). Mix well until the paste is smooth.

Slowly add the washing-soda solution to the indigo paste in the jar and stir well until the indigo paste has completely dissolved, and no gritty particles remain. Take particular care when using natural indigo.

Put four litres or one gallon of water at a temperature of 50°C (120°F) into a stainless-steel dyepan, or heat until this temperature is reached.

*Indigo on cotton yarn, boiled in
iron solution afterwards.*

45

Do not allow the temperature to exceed 60°C (140°F) at any time.

Gently stir the indigo/washing-soda solution into the water in the dyepan, making sure that it is well mixed in.

Now sprinkle 25g sodium dithionite (or 15g *Thiox* or 25g colour-run-remover) over the surface of the liquid in the dyepan and leave for thirty to sixty minutes, keeping the temperature constant. After this time the liquid in the dyepan should have changed colour – from blue to a greeny-yellow. The surface of the liquid may remain blue, as this is in contact with air and will be reacting with oxygen.

The blue film can be removed with kitchen paper before adding the material to be dyed. A few drops of neutral pH detergent will help disperse it and also help the indigo to penetrate the fibres. If the vat still appears blue, add a little more of your chosen reducing agent and leave it for a further five to ten minutes. When all the blue has gone, the vat is ready for use.

If you are dyeing wool or silk, keep the temperature constant at 50°C (120°F). If you are dyeing cotton or linen, let the vat cool to 30°C (86°F) before use.

Gently immerse the yarn or fabric, which should be well wetted but squeezed to remove excess water. Do not put more material in the vat than will lie easily below the surface, as any sections left above the surface will be blotchy. Leave the yarn or fabric in the vat for five to fifteen minutes.

Now remove the material very gently, making sure that it does not drip into the vat. Keep a plastic bowl beside the vat to take the material as you remove it. At this stage the material will be a yellow-green colour. If there are any spots of undissolved indigo on the material when it is taken from the vat, plunge it briefly into a bucket of water to remove them, or they may cause blotches.

Expose the material to the air for ten to fifteen minutes to oxidise, gently separating the strands to ensure that air penetrates all the way through. You will see the material gradually turning blue. You can build up the depth of colour by redipping the material in the vat and then airing it again, until you achieve the desired shade.

If the vat begins to turn blue, add a little more reducing agent, but only enough to turn it yellow-green again.

Thiox will not dissolve in water that is cooler than 50°C (120°F), so dissolve it first in plenty of hot water if you are using a cool vat. When you have the desired depth of colour, rinse the material thoroughly, adding a cupful of white vinegar to the final rinse. Then wash well in soapy water and rinse well again.

When the material no longer takes up any colour, or if the vat has turned completely blue, then the vat is exhausted and you will need to make a fresh one for further batches of material. Before disposal of the spent dyebath, fully exhaust the dye potential by leaving a piece of old cotton sheeting (or something similar) in it overnight. Exhaust any remaining reducing agent by whisking or agitating the vat to incorporate oxygen from the air into it.

Yeast fermentation method

This method is not entirely foolproof, takes a long time to complete and tends to be rather smelly. However, it does have the advantage of requiring fewer chemicals. The following instructions are for a 4.5-litre (1-gallon) vat.

Fill the pan with water at 38°C (100°F), and add two tablespoons of sugar and two packets of dried yeast. Stir well, and leave until the yeast begins to froth and bubble.

Meanwhile, dissolve two tablespoons of washing soda in hot water and add two tablespoons of natural indigo (or one tablespoon of synthetic indigo), stirring well to make sure that the indigo has completely dissolved.

Add this indigo mixture to the yeast solution in the pan and then place the pan in a warm place to ferment, covering it with a well-fitting lid or some cling film. The warm place may be over a pilot light of a gas cooker or on an electric plate warmer. The temperature must be kept constant, but it must not be allowed to exceed 50°C (120°F).

Fermentation may take forty-eight hours with natural indigo, but is usually somewhat quicker when you use synthetic indigo. Fermentation is complete when the liquid in the vat has become yellow-green in colour.

The vat can now be used in the same way as described earlier, but remember that this method does not require the addition of a reducing agent or colour-run-remover. Simply add the yarn gently, leave for forty-five minutes to an hour, then remove carefully and air.

Woad *Isatis tinctoria*

This plant, which has been used for centuries as a dyestuff, is one of the few that gives a blue colour. The fresh leaves from the first year's growth are used in this recipe and the depth of colour can be adjusted according to the amount of leaves used. 400 per cent dry weight of leaves to 100 per cent dry weight of material will give relatively deep shades.

Some of the lovely shades of blue you can get with woad on wool and cotton.

For success with woad you must use soft water (rainwater, for example). You will also need some washing soda or household ammonia and reducing agent, as for indigo.

Making the dyebath

Tear the leaves into small pieces and put them in a plastic bucket or dyepan. Pour boiling soft water over the leaves, enough for the dyebath that you require.

Leave the leaves to steep for twenty to thirty minutes, then strain off the sherry-coloured liquid, squeezing the leaves to extract all the dye. The leaves can be kept and reused for a further dyebath, giving you a tan colour.

Put the strained liquid into a bucket or dyepan and add a little washing soda or a few drops of household ammonia to turn the liquid a dark-green colour. Aerate this mixture by whisking it vigorously or by pouring it from one bucket to another for about fifteen minutes, until the fresh froth that is formed has turned blue and is beginning to turn green or yellow again.

Heat the liquid in a dyepan to a temperature of 50°C (120°F), then slowly sprinkle approximately one teaspoon of reducing agent over the surface to remove the oxygen. Do not stir.

Leave the liquid to stand, keeping the temperature at 50°C (120°F) for about five to fifteen minutes. Then gently add the wetted wool (or cotton), which does not require mordanting, taking care not to disturb the the surface too much. Leave the material to soak for twenty to thirty minutes. Then remove it very carefully and without letting it drip into the dyepan.

Air the material for twenty to thirty minutes; during this time it will turn from yellow to blue. Dip and air alternately until the dyepan is exhausted or until you have got the depth of colour you need. Then rinse well and wash in soapy water. Rinse again to remove the soap.

Dyeing with the used woad leaves

You can use unmordanted wool; otherwise pre-mordant the wool with alum and cream of tartar. Alternatively, you can add the mordant to the dyepan for a 'simultaneous' dyebath. Put the wool into a dyepan with the woad leaves and simmer for about an hour. This will produce pinky-tan shades.

Storing woad

It is also possible to make a woad solution for storage. To do this, put the torn-up leaves in a plastic container which has a tightly fitting lid. (Ice-cream containers or lidded plastic paint buckets are ideal, but make sure you clean them out thoroughly first!)

Pour boiling soft water over the leaves until the container is full to the brim so as to exclude any air, then put the lid on tightly and leave for forty minutes.

Strain off the sherry-coloured liquid into another container and gradually add washing soda (or ammonia) until the liquid turns dark green. Whisk the liquid thoroughly until the fresh froth no longer turns blue. Now pour the liquid into an airtight container, filling it completely so it overflows slightly. (A large sweet jar with a screw-top lid is ideal for this.) Add one teaspoonful of sodium metabisulphite as a preservative and screw the lid down tightly.

A woad solution made in this way can sometimes be stored successfully for several years. To use the stored solution, put it into a dyepan, heat it to 50°C (120°F) and carry on as for fresh woad-leaf solution. Exhaust the woad vat as described for indigo (see page 46) before disposing of the solution.

Woad on woollen fleece.

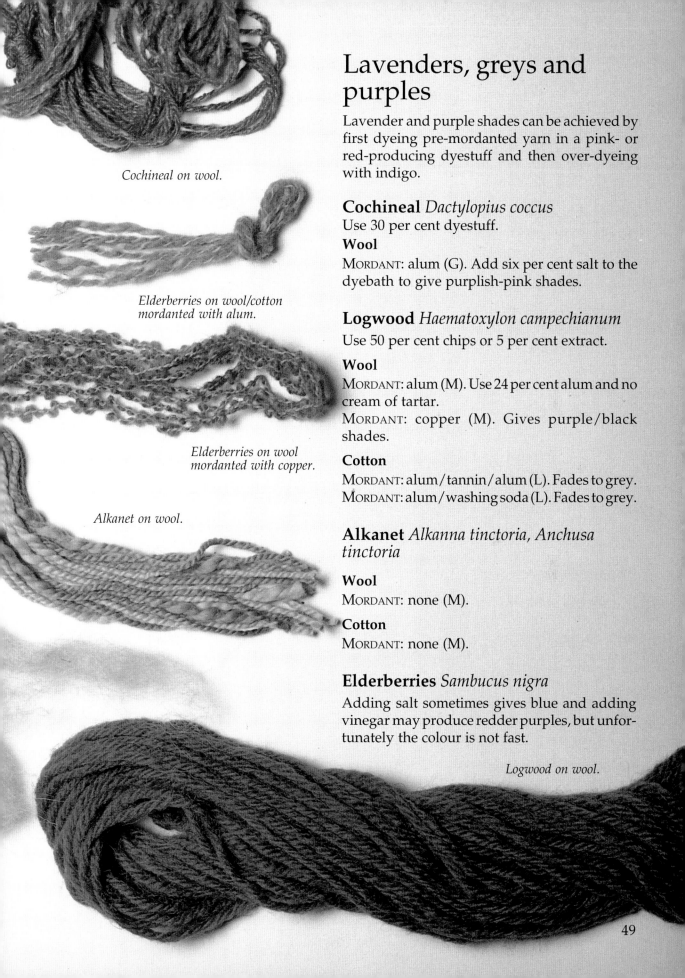

Cochineal on wool.

Elderberries on wool/cotton mordanted with alum.

Elderberries on wool mordanted with copper.

Alkanet on wool.

Lavenders, greys and purples

Lavender and purple shades can be achieved by first dyeing pre-mordanted yarn in a pink- or red-producing dyestuff and then over-dyeing with indigo.

Cochineal *Dactylopius coccus*

Use 30 per cent dyestuff.

Wool

MORDANT: alum (G). Add six per cent salt to the dyebath to give purplish-pink shades.

Logwood *Haematoxylon campechianum*

Use 50 per cent chips or 5 per cent extract.

Wool

MORDANT: alum (M). Use 24 per cent alum and no cream of tartar.
MORDANT: copper (M). Gives purple/black shades.

Cotton

MORDANT: alum/tannin/alum (L). Fades to grey.
MORDANT: alum/washing soda (L). Fades to grey.

Alkanet *Alkanna tinctoria, Anchusa tinctoria*

Wool

MORDANT: none (M).

Cotton

MORDANT: none (M).

Elderberries *Sambucus nigra*

Adding salt sometimes gives blue and adding vinegar may produce redder purples, but unfortunately the colour is not fast.

Logwood on wool.

Pinks and reds

Cochineal *Dactylopius coccus*

Use 25–50 per cent dyestuff. No mordant is needed.

Prepare the dyebath in the usual way, then add a small amount of citric acid (half a teaspoon) or some lemon juice to turn the dyebath red in colour. Then dye the wool in the usual way. For a stronger dyebath, you could grind the cochineal to a powder in a coffee grinder and simmer it to dissolve the dye colour. Remember to clean the coffee grinder well afterwards, or your coffee may have an unusual colour and taste!

Wool

MORDANT: copper (G). Gives a dusky pink.
MORDANT: alum (G).

Cotton

Use 25–50 per cent dyestuff.
MORDANT: alum/tannin/alum (M).
MORDANT: alum/washing soda (M).

For red you could also try this dye-mixing recipe:

20 per cent cochineal + 50 per cent weld + 6 per cent salt.

Cochineal on cotton.

Safflower on cotton.

Cochineal on wool.

Cochineal on cotton.

Cochineal on wool.

Reused safflower on cotton.

Safflower on silk.

Safflower on cotton.

Safflower

As well as producing yellow, safflower petals will also produce pink on cotton and silk yarn or cloth. The colour is a shocking pink, but it is not very light-fast. It was the original dye colour used on the ribbon tied around legal documents – hence the term 'red tape'.

Dyeing cotton and silk pink

The yarn or cloth does not need to be mordanted. Allow 200 per cent dry weight of safflower petals to dry weight of yarn or cloth. You will also need a supply of soft water, some potassium carbonate (or soda or ammonia), some dilute acetic acid (or lemon juice) and a few pH indicators.

Tie the petals securely in a piece of muslin and extract the natural yellow dye by squeezing the muslin bag under cold running water until the water runs clear. Wear rubber gloves or your hands will become yellow. This process can take a long time, so be prepared.

When the petals no longer yield any more yellow dye, squeeze out all the excess water. Remove the petals from the muslin and put them in a pan or plastic container.

Cover the petals with cold, soft water, sufficient for your subsequent dyebath. Gradually add potassium carbonate (or washing soda) until the petals turn red: at this stage the water should be pH 11. Leave to steep for one hour, then squeeze the petals well and strain them off. You can keep the petals and use them again for paler shades.

Add one to two teaspoons of dilute acetic acid or lemon juice to bring the dye liquid down to pH 6. Now the dye liquid is a bright red and is ready for use.

Do not heat the dye liquid – use it cold. Add the yarn or cloth and leave it to steep in the dye liquid overnight. In the morning the yarn or cloth should be a lovely bright pink. Rinse well.

Deeper shades can be achieved by using a higher percentage of safflower petals. The discarded petals can often be reused in the same way for paler shades.

Madder *Rubia tinctorum*

Wool
MORDANT: copper (G). Gives a browny-pink/red.
MORDANT: alum (G).

Cotton
MORDANT: alum/tannin/alum (G).
MORDANT: alum/washing soda (G).

Madder is one of the most light-fast of natural dyes and has been in use for over 5,000 years. It is usually available as chopped root and sometimes as a powder. The powder is not always as reliable as the chopped root because it is not easy to tell if it has been adulterated with some other substance such as brickdust.

With different mordants, madder will give good fast colours ranging from salmon pink (with copper) to bright red (with alum). Used without a mordant, it will give coral to rust shades. Reddish-brown shades can be obtained when iron, in the form of ferrous sulphate, is used as a modifier. Adding citric acid (or lemon juice) to the dyebath before adding the material gives orange shades on unmordanted and alum-mordanted wool.

Making the dyebath
Put the chopped madder root in the dyebath. If the dyestuff is in powder form, mix it with a little water and add this solution to the dyebath. Fill the dyebath with the required amount of water and then add the wool or cotton to be dyed. You will get better shades if the material is left in the dyebath together with the dyestuff. However, if you are using chopped root you will have to shake the pieces free from the fibres after dyeing, whereas good-quality fine powder will almost dissolve in the dyebath. Leave to soak overnight, then continue the dyeing process as described opposite.

Madder on wool top mordanted with alum.

Madder on silk.

Madder on cotton mordanted with alum and washing soda.

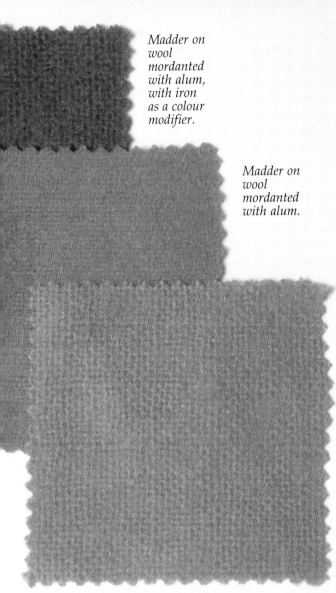

Madder on wool mordanted with alum, with iron as a colour modifier.

Madder on wool mordanted with alum.

Madder on wool mordanted with alum.

Dyeing wool

Slowly bring the temperature of the dyebath up to 60°C (140°F) and hold it at this temperature for one hour. Madder should never be boiled with wool in the dyebath as only rust-brown shades will result. Leave the wool to cool in the dyebath.

For deeper shades repeat the process. If the colour is still not deep enough, remove the wool and boil the madder vigorously for thirty minutes. Strain off the liquid, leave it to cool down and then put the material back in the dyebath. Raise the temperature as above and hold at this level for another hour.

Dyeing cotton

Bring the dyebath slowly to the boil and then simmer for forty-five minutes. Leave the cotton in the dyebath and repeat the process as necessary to achieve deeper shades. Rinse well and wash.

Exhausting the dye potential

Further colour can be extracted from the used dyebath solution. Remove the material from the dyebath and return any chopped root shaken from the fibres to the dyepan. Add more water if necessary and then boil the madder vigorously for forty-five minutes to extract the remaining dye potential. Strain off the dye liquid, leave it to cool, and then use this batch to dye material as described above. Alternatively, add some citric acid to produce orange shades; the acid will help to exhaust any dye potential remaining.

Madder on wool (not boiled), on a rhubarb base + citric acid.

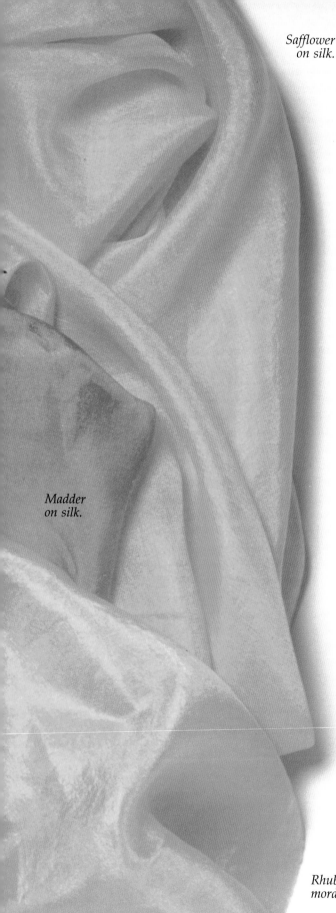

Safflower on silk.

Madder on silk.

Oranges, rusts, and browns

Annatto
This will produce warm orange shades.

Cutch *Acacia catechu*
Wool
MORDANT: alum (M).
Cotton
MORDANT: use any of the three cotton mordanting recipes (M).

Henna *Lawsonia inermis*
Use 50 per cent dyestuff. You will get rust to tan shades.
Wool
MORDANT: none (M).
Cotton
MORDANT: alum/tannin/alum (M).
MORDANT: alum/washing soda (M).

Lichen (various species)
Wool
MORDANT: none (G).

Onion skins *Allium cepa*
Use 30 per cent dyestuff for wool and 50 to 60 per cent dyestuff for cotton.
Cotton
MORDANT: use any of the cotton mordanting recipes (M).

Weld *Reseda luteola*
Wool
MORDANT: copper (G).

Cochineal
Add citric acid to get rusty-red shades.

Rhubarb root and washing soda on silk (no mordant) – cold soak only.

Annatto on wool mordanted with alum.

Madder exhaust on wool (no mordant) + citric acid.

Cochineal on wool (no mordant) + citric acid.

Onion skins on wool mordanted with rhubarb leaves.

Madder on wool (not boiled) mordanted with rhubarb leaves.

Walnut hulls *Juglans regia*

Wool

MORDANT: none (G).

Cotton

MORDANT: none (M).

Black walnut leaves *Juglans nigra*

Gives tan shades.

Wool

MORDANT: none (G).

Cotton

MORDANT: none (M).
MORDANT: alum/tannin/alum (M).
MORDANT: alum/washing soda (M).

Iron

Treat the material in the iron solution, following either the hot or the cold method described above for yellow. Remove the fabric and squeeze it but do not rinse.

Work the material in a hot solution (50–82°C (120–180°F)) of two teaspoons of washing soda per litre of water. Squeeze and then air, opening the fabric as described on page 41 for yellow. The colour will change to orange or rust. Repeat the process for deeper shades, using the same iron and washing-soda solutions. Then rinse, wash well and rinse again.

Madder

Adding half to one teaspoon of citric acid (or the juice of one or two lemons) stirred in well before the material is added gives orange shades on unmordanted and alum-mordanted wool.

Adding half to one teaspoon of ferrous sulphate, stirred in well towards the end of the dyeing process (remembering to remove the wool first), gives a reddish brown if the dyed wool is replaced in the dyebath for five minutes. See pages 52–53 for general instructions on how to use madder.

Woad on woollen fleece (see page 48).

Walnut hulls on wool.

Madder on silk mordanted with alum, with iron as a colour modifier.

Madder on wool mordanted with alum, with iron as a colour modifier.

Cutch on cotton mordanted with alum.

Logwood on silk mordanted with copper.

Iron on cotton mordanted with tannin.

Madder on wool mordanted with alum, with iron as a colour modifier.

Logwood on silk mordanted with copper.

Alkanet on silk (no mordant).

Iron and tannin on silk.

Black and neutral colours

It is not easy to get a true black using natural dyes, although logwood over-dyed with indigo often produces a colour which is very close to black. In the past, black was often obtained by boiling yarn or cloth first in an oak-gall solution and then in an iron solution, after which it would frequently be over-dyed in other dyebaths until black was achieved. The combination of tannin (in this case from oak galls) and iron was, and in some parts of the world still is, a common source of black for vegetable fibres. Cotton pre-mordanted with tannin alone and then dyed with walnut hulls and iron as a modifier will give almost black shades with a good light-fastness.

For black try these over-dyeing recipes:

Walnut hulls + iron, over-dyed with indigo
Logwood + iron, over-dyed with indigo
Cutch over-dyed with indigo
Onion skins, over-dyed in cochineal or logwood, then over-dyed with indigo.

You could also try mixing the following dye-stuffs:

30 per cent logwood + 30 per cent fustic + 10 per cent madder (with iron as a modifier).

Iron/tannin

Mordant cotton and silk with tannin as described on page 30.

Simmer the mordanted material in the iron solution for about fifteen minutes or work it for thirty minutes in a cool iron solution. Repeat the process for deeper shades. Rinse, wash and rinse again.

The dyer's favourites – some plants to grow

While it is possible to obtain all the important dyestuffs mentioned in this book, except woad, from dyestuff suppliers, there is a lot of fun in growing your own dye-plants. A fairly wide range of colours can be obtained from quite a small number of plants.

If you intend to dye vast quantities of yarn or cloth, you would need a very large garden to grow enough for your needs; but for the craft-dyer who wishes to produce only a few naturally dyed items each year, and who is prepared to devote a part of the garden to plants which are useful but not always particularly decorative, there is considerable scope.

The most useful plants to grow in your garden are: woad for blues and tans; madder for reds and corals; and weld for yellows and golds. When you combine the colours from two or more of these plants, you can get greens, oranges, purples and even black. You can, of course, grow many of the other dyestuffs mentioned in this book to give added variety and colour to your garden.

Planning

Bear in mind the growth habits of the plants, particularly those of madder, weld and woad. I would recommend growing these three plants in blocks, as their growth is easier to control that way, especially as madder roots should not be disturbed for three to five years, except when dividing some of the plants.

Madder is one of the few reliable sources of red, and you should devote as much space as you can to this useful plant.

Both weld and woad plants can be left to self-seed, but this will not guarantee plants growing where you want them.

Madder *Rubia tinctorum*

Madder is a perennial plant and produces jointed stalks which grow to quite a length. The stalks are covered in fine hairs which make them rough and sticky to the touch (rather like goosegrass or cleavers), and, as the stems are not very strong, they need staking (unless you allow them to creep over the ground). The stalks will die off each year, but the roots, which are the parts used for dyeing, continue to grow and spread, producing fresh shoots above ground each year.

Madder seeds should be sown during March in pots or seed trays (indoors) or under glass (outdoors). If necessary, transplant the seedlings to larger pots so the roots can grow unrestricted.

When the plants are strong enough, in June or July, plant them out where they are to grow permanently, allowing 45cm² (18sq in) per plant.

Madder grows best in full sun and well-drained, well-limed soil, with plenty of compost and manure.

Madder roots are not harvested for dyeing until the plants are three years old. However, if you want to enlarge your madder bed, the plants can be lifted during May of the second year, divided, and then replanted. Make sure you dig deeply, so that you do not damage the roots, which do tend to creep, and keep as much soil around them as possible. Water them well after replanting, and continue watering until new shoots appear.

New root growth can be encouraged by laying the madder tops on the ground and putting soil on each one, at a leaf joint, and pressing it gently into the ground, rather as one does with strawberry runners.

From the third year of growth onwards, you can dig up the madder roots in August for dyeing. If you divide and replant some of the roots regularly, and also encourage the madder tops to produce new roots, you should have a permanent supply of madder. In the third year of growth some plants should develop tiny yellow flowers followed by berries. When mature, the berries become black and look like black peppercorns. Each contains one or two seeds which can be dried for sowing fresh madder crops.

How to dry madder
Wash the roots well; this will remove some of the brown and yellow pigments which can make the dye colour dull. Dry them thoroughly in a damp-free place, either on newspaper or on wire-mesh racks, or you could simply lay them out in the sun to dry. They can also be dried out on racks in a very cool oven.

When they are thoroughly dried, they are usually brittle enough to break into small pieces, or you can try chopping them, although this is not easy. (Some people also grind their madder roots in a coffee-grinder or blender). Store the madder pieces in paper bags in a dry place for later use.

It is also possible to use fresh madder roots. They should be chopped into tiny pieces and blended into a paste in a blender or with a pestle and mortar.

Weld *Reseda luteola*

Weld, a biennial plant, grows up to 1m (3ft) high before flowering and the whole top is cut for dyeing, so some plants need to be left in the ground to produce seeds for harvesting the following year.

Sow the seeds outside in rows during September or October. In the following spring, when the seedlings are 50–75mm (2–3in) high, thin or transplant them 225mm (9in) apart, taking care not to damage the tap root.

Madder: a sticky, creeping plant, indispensable in your dye-garden.

Weld in autumn, showing the seeds.

Weld in flower.

In June or July of the same year the plants, standing about 1m (3ft) high, will have produced flowering stalks. These are cut off at ground level and the whole plant-top used for dyeing.

Weld tops can be used fresh or they can be dried for later use. If you cut some stalks off just above the lowest side shoots, these will continue to grow and can be harvested later in the year. You can continue to harvest weld through until about September.

Leave one or two plants untouched and these will flower and produce seeds around September. The tiny black seeds are encased in small green pods down the flowering shoot and they can be shaken out on to paper, rather like poppy seeds, and either sown immediately or stored in a dry place for sowing the following year.

Self-sown weld seeds often produce rosettes of leaves in late autumn/early winter and these will over-winter hardily and produce flowering shoots the following year.

When you have harvested the seeds and cut off the plant-tops for dyeing, dig up all the plants and sow seed for next year's crop.

How to dry weld
Hang the plant-tops upside down to dry in a dark, damp-free place, allowing plenty of air to circulate around them. When they are quite dry and brittle, chop or break them into small pieces and store them in paper bags in a dry place.

Woad *Isatis tinctoria*

Woad, too, is a biennial plant, although it can be grown as an annual if the seed is sown in February or March.

As woad plants do not produce seeds in the first year, you will need to buy enough for two years' sowing. However, if you leave two or three plants alone they will mature in the second year, when you can harvest your own seeds.

Sow the seeds outside in rows during October for early crops (June onwards) or during February/March for later harvesting. When the

Wood in flower.

plants are 50–75mm (2–3in) high, thin them out or transplant them about 300mm (12in) apart, taking care not to damage the tap root.

Leaves for dyeing harvested after October will not yield much colour. The plants form a rosette of leaves, rather like spinach. The leaves should be carefully picked off close to the ground. You will probably find that some plants will continue to produce leaves right through the growing season.

Woad leaves should be used fresh for dyeing, or you can make them into a woad solution for storing, as described on page 48.

When you have harvested all the leaves, dig up the roots to allow space for next year's crop.

Plants left in place to mature will reach about 1.75m (5ft) and will flower the following April and May, producing a mass of most attractive yellow flowers, which then develop black seeds. Harvest the seeds in July and August.

Cut off the seed heads plus their stems and stack them upright in a dry place to dry and mature. When they are quite dry and brittle, remove the seeds and store them in paper bags.

If stored bone dry, woad seeds remain viable for up to five years. So if you have a particularly large harvest of seeds one year, you may have enough for the next two or three years, which means you can dig up all your woad plants that year, leaving more space for the next year's plants.

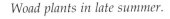

Woad seeds.

Woad plants in late summer.

Japanese indigo in a pot.

Japanese indigo *Polygonum tinctorium*

This member of the buckwheat family grows happily in a pot, but will need bringing into a warm place indoors for the winter as it is not frost-hardy and will need some warmth to flower and produce seeds from November to January. The seeds should be removed with tweezers when they have turned black, then dried for sowing again indoors or under glass in spring. It germinates readily and some seedlings can be planted about 20–30cm (8–12in) apart (closer in pots) in early summer, in the garden in rich soil – but keep some in pots to flower indoors for next year. The plants need plenty of water.

The leaves can be harvested from July to late September and used fresh or dried, or frozen for later use. They are used as woad leaves for good light-fast blues; *however,* do *not* pour boiling water on them as for woad, but add cold water and bring the leaves slowly to just below simmering point, then turn off the heat and let the leaves steep for one hour. Then pour off the sherry-coloured liquid and proceed as for woad solution on page 48.

Dyer's broom *Genista tinctoria*

Dyer's broom is a hardy perennial which is also very attractive, with its display of yellow flowers. It will grow in most situations. Seeds should be sown outdoors in autumn and seedlings planted out in spring, 60cm (2ft) apart.

The whole plant tops should be harvested for dyeing when the yellow flowers appear. The plants will produce more growth and can often be harvested again later in the year, so cut them back to the lowest growth shoots. The harvested tops can be cut and dried for later use or used fresh.

With alum mordant: reasonable (medium) light-fastness.

With copper mordant: good light-fastness.

With iron mordant: good light-fastness.

Safflower *Carthamus tinctoria*

This unusual-looking and decorative plant, much sought after by flower-dryers and arrangers, is indispensable for a range of striking pinks (unfortunately of limited light-fastness). Sow it outdoors in rows in late spring or early summer.

A long hot summer is usually necessary to produce flowers. The tiny petals are the parts used for dyeing and these can be harvested and dried for use when you have managed to collect enough for a dyebath. Safflower will produce strong yellows on wool and paler yellows on cotton. You can get pinks and corals on silk and cotton (but not on wool) by following the recipe on page 51.

Rhubarb *Rheum species*

Rhubarb leaves make a useful natural mordant, while the roots can be used as a dyestuff to get golden-yellow to mustard shades. Grow it in any rich soil following your usual method. When you harvest the stalks for eating, remove the leaves to use as a mordant or a dyestuff. The roots can be used fresh or dried and should be chopped up or pounded before use, or finely ground if they have been dried.

Good light-fastness – no mordant required.

Safflower.

Dyer's broom.

Glossary

After-mordants   After-mordants are substances, usually iron or copper, applied immediately after dyeing to enhance the colours.

Assistant   Assistants are substances used with mordants to help them do their job properly.

Dyestuff   This is what we call the source of colour: various plants, woods, roots, flowers, etc.

Fugitive colour   A colour that does not remain in the yarn or fabric after dyeing but fades or washes out.

Mordanting   Mordanting is the process of pre-treatment of fibres which allows the applied dye colour to be permanently fixed.

Mordants   These substances are used to fix a dye permanently to the fibres, improve the take-up of the dye colour, and enhance light- and wash-fastness. They are used in solution, often with the addition of an 'assistant' which improves the fixing of the mordant to the fibre.

Over-dyeing   Over-dyeing, also known as bottoming or top-dyeing, is probably the best way of creating colours that are unobtainable from single dyestuffs.

Scouring   This means getting wool completely clean and free from grease or dirt before mordanting by soaking it overnight in a solution of liquid detergent.

Substantive dyes   Dyestuffs that will fix without the use of a mordant are known as 'substantive' dyes.

Index